VIKING

THE ESSENTIALS OF WORLD RELIGIONS

Trilochan Sastry is professor at Indian Institute of Management (IIM) Bangalore and a former dean of the institute. He did his BTech from Indian Institute of Technology Delhi, MBA from IIM Ahmedabad and PhD from Massachusetts Institute of Technology. He is the founder of Association for Democratic Reforms, an NGO that works on electoral and political reforms, and also of Centre for Collective Development and Farmveda, which works with tens of thousands of small farmers. Sastry has received various awards for his academic work and his contribution to society. He has been interested in religion since early adolescence and has lived in monasteries, studied the sacred texts, attended classes with various teachers and visited several pilgrimage sites. His previous book, *The Essentials of Hinduism*, was well received and is widely popular.

THE
ESSENTIALS
of

....

WORLD
RELIGIONS

....

An Underlying Harmony

....

TRILOCHAN
SASTRY

PENGUIN
VIKING

An imprint of Penguin Random House

VIKING

Viking is an imprint of the Penguin Random House group of companies
whose addresses can be found at global.penguinrandomhouse.com

Published by Penguin Random House India Pvt. Ltd
4th Floor, Capital Tower 1, MG Road,
Gurugram 122 002, Haryana, India

Penguin
Random House
India

First published in Viking by Penguin Random House India 2024

10 9 8 7 6 5 4 3 2 1

ISBN 9780143466888

Typeset in Adobe Garamond Pro by Manipal Technologies Limited, Manipal
Printed at Thomson Press India Ltd, New Delhi

www.penguin.co.in

Om, Amen, Amin

Most sacred syllables of Hinduism, Buddhism, Jainism, Sikhism (Om); Christianity (Amen); Judaism and Islam (Amin)

CONTENTS

PREFACE

A question that many people ask is whether different religions have anything in common. Many are curious about their own religion but have not had the inclination to study it themselves. They depend on popularly available (but not entirely accurate) material, what they see around them, the customs and traditions in their families and the stories they have heard to form their view of the religion they are born into. Hence, many people's knowledge of their own religion is limited. Their knowledge of other religions is even more limited. But most people have strong opinions on religion nevertheless, whether it is the one they believe in or that of others. Even agnostics and atheists usually have strong views on religion. If such opinions are based on partial information, they can lead to various problems in society.

In this introductory book, we examine all the great religions. This is not an easy task, so we have set some boundaries. For many, social customs and rituals define religion. But these customs and rituals are derived from the sacred texts and from the social contexts in which these religions originated. These are different for different religions. For instance, dress codes and even hairstyles differ. Foods that are allowed or forbidden differ. There are various ways of praying or worshipping. Many follow the rituals and dress codes but are not aware of the essential teachings of their religious texts. Nevertheless, they may be devout and are considered religious. Rituals, rites and dress codes differ widely across religions. They help many believers to practice their own religion.

But do the social, ritual and mundane aspects reflect the essential Truths of a religion? What is the source of a religion? All religions say that their founders* received revelations from a higher or inner source or from God. For example, the rishis of the Vedic times, Buddha, Mahavira, the Abrahamic prophets common to Judaism, Christianity and Islam, and Jesus, Zarathustra, Mohammad and Guru Nanak are either the earliest teachers or founders of the great religions of the world. Every religion claims that its sacred texts are based on the revelations received by these teachers and founders. These texts are given the highest authority. The essence of any religion is contained in these

---

* Judaism and Hinduism are not based on one founder. They are based on the teachings of several prophets and rishis. But they also have sacred texts.

sacred texts. It is deeper than the external rituals, dress codes, food habits and methods of worship.

So any search for a common ground has to go back to the original sacred texts. Since the sacred texts are available, anyone can study them. However, most of them are in languages that are no longer spoken. Translations are available in various languages, but the texts themselves are very voluminous. Over the centuries, the original teachings as laid down in the sacred texts were slowly forgotten, as most people do not read them. It is often left to the priests to interpret them. Even today, only a handful of serious scholars and devout followers are aware of the essence of their religions.

However, even a casual reading reveals a lot of common ground. For instance, all religions preach peace and love. All have very similar dos and don'ts that define good conduct. The limited study in this book is about the essentials of the religions of the world as anyone can discover in the sacred texts. A careful study reveals that at the spiritual level, there is much that is common. We highlight this aspect. Where there are differences in philosophy, these are presented as well. The rituals in different religions are not examined here. They are far too complex for anyone to study.

Why is this study important? Down the ages, religion has played an important role in the lives of individuals and nations. Those who follow the basic tenets of their religion derive some benefit. At the same time, it has given rise to conflicts, wars and bloodshed. In times of crisis, religion becomes even more important as we look for ways of overcoming our problems. We are at a unique point in history in the twenty-first century. Religious tensions and conflicts continue the world over. This leads to greater assertion of religion-based identities. Periodic economic slowdowns, religious and political extremism and climate change are three of the major issues we grapple with today. Economic slowdowns lead to joblessness. Extremism leads to violence. Climate change leads to problems in agriculture and in the environment and affects the livelihood of millions of farmers. All this leads to anxiety and uncertainty. Religion becomes a support for many in times of crisis. Anxiety and uncertainty give rise to various types of politics, governments, political leaders and their followers. Religion is often invoked for political purposes, leading to inevitable conflict.

To the three factors mentioned above, we can add two more. More people have migrated today from one part of the world to another than perhaps ever before in history. There are perhaps more migrants today than the entire population of the world in the late seventeenth century. People of various races, religions and cultures often live together. In good times, this is probably good as it breaks down prejudices. But in crises, it also has the potential for conflict. Another historically new development is the information and digital revolution. The ordinary person has never had access to as much information as today. Within seconds, news of any event anywhere in the world can reach the remotest corners of the globe. Both accurate information and fake news have multiplied. Unfortunately, the way we are made, bad news is remembered more often, and we are unable to separate accurate news from fake. During crises, our doubts and fears surface and we naturally latch onto real and imaginary dangers. Conflicts are no longer between nations, races and religions. Instant communication, fake news and hate speeches have divided communities, groups that were earlier undivided and even families, relatives and friends. Many then look for stability in religion and in our political leaders.

The seeds of conflict no longer lie merely in politics, religion, leaders or crises. These seeds are now present in the minds of 'ordinary' people. To resolve these conflicts sometimes seems impossible. Crises of various kinds lead many to revert to religion (or abandon it) or some ideology. Unfortunately, it also leads to suspicion of other religions and ideologies. As a possible solution, Arnold Toynbee, the author of the twelve-volume *A Study of History*, said '. . . (a) harmony of religions . . . can make it possible for the human race to grow together into a single family—and, in the Atomic Age, this is the only alternative to destroying ourselves.'[1]

This is the basic need that the book tries to address. A look at the essentials of religion can remove one source of conflict that is based on a suspicion of other religions—if not from the world, at least from our own mind. Modern discourse is based on politics and economics. Modern science and technology views religion as either irrelevant or a nuisance to be dealt with that will hopefully go away as people become more rational. However, a majority of people around the world believe in God. This is true even in the West, where church attendance has steadily declined, but belief in God has not declined that much. In the modern era, when hundreds of millions around the world daily come into contact with people of other faiths, there is a need for the public discourse to include religion. The simple reason is that it is too important to be ignored. Whether one accepts religion or not, whether one thinks one's own religion is the best or has a more liberal view, accepting all religions, we cannot live in silos anymore. Informed opinion about all religions is perhaps critical today.

A companion book called *The Essentials of Hinduism* examines the essentials of that religion. This book examines the common ground between different religions. If this helps anyone think and understand more about religion, make an informed choice about what to accept and what to leave out, it will have served its purpose.[2]

INTRODUCTION

There is a difference between what a religion says and how it is understood and practised. Religion is understood by most of us through our own life experiences from childhood. Our family, the rituals we are exposed to, the stories we read and hear, the teachings from respected elders and priests and some reading of the texts determine our view of the religion we are born into. Most people do not read the original texts. Priests of all religions influence a large number of religious people. But there may be a difference between what the priest says and the texts of that religion. This leads to an incomplete understanding of one's own religion.

Modern science and technology give primacy to reason and explain most phenomena we encounter in everyday life. For many, the need for religion and God is replaced by reason and science. As a result, regular attendance in churches has gone down, especially in the West. People then end up believing that the essential aspects of religion are going to a temple, a church or a mosque, and the social norms, marriage rituals, death ceremonies, observing holy days through fasting or feasting, chanting sacred prayers, reading portions of some texts and so on. For those who are more scientifically minded or value reason, all these seem old-fashioned and archaic, and they reject religion.

However, the essence of a religion comes from its founders and prophets. Without exception, all the religions say that their founders were enlightened and received direct revelations from God, or an inner or higher source, or discovered a higher truth.* What they said has become scripture or sacred. These sacred texts are considered the highest authority in any religion.

Even a casual reading of the sacred texts of any religion shows that the words of the founders have little to do with what is popularly understood as religion. However, they spoke in the language of those times to better communicate with the general public. We need to understand the context of those times when studying these texts. For instance, we read of various animals—cows, donkeys, camels, foxes, birds and so on—in these texts, which we do not encounter in our daily life today. The parables are from a social context that is no longer relevant. So a proper reading would have to go back to the essence, the 'meaning of the meaning',

---

* Buddhism is agnostic about God and Jainism is atheistic. So we use the phrase 'God or Truth' to include all the religions.

as it is sometimes said. Buddha left his palace and went into the 'homeless' state. Christ says, 'Foxes have holes and birds have nests, but the Son of Man has no place to lay his head.' Both are in essence saying or doing the same thing—leaving everything in search of God or Truth. Buddha's Four Noble Truths are said to be the essence of Buddhism. But if you go to various Buddhist temples, the rituals practised have little to do with Buddha's teachings.

All the great religions developed elaborate philosophies or theologies down the ages, but various sects broke away and created further divisions. Many philosophical texts were written. The various philosophical texts even within one religion can differ among themselves. Unlike the revelations that are considered divine or supersensory, these philosophies use the human mind to establish a doctrine. We focus on the original texts revealed to the founders and not so much on these philosophies.

For most, knowledge of other religions is even more limited than knowledge of their own. Rituals and festivals of other religions may seem strange to us. Based on all this and hearsay, we develop some notions of other religions. Here again, the answer lies in reading their holy books to gain a clearer understanding. One religious student was told by his teacher to read the sacred texts of other religions. He was told to underline what made sense and to ignore the rest. The reason is that we sometimes find the texts of other religions strange. The language, parables and customs are often very different. More than one's own religion, it is even more important that we try to understand the meaning of the meaning when reading about the other great religions.

Critics of religion point to the violence, bloodshed and wars fought in the name of religion, the incalculable suffering over the centuries that people have undergone, and hence reject both religion and God. They also point to the triumph of science and reason, that explains most things, and ask, where is God? Such arguments do not change the minds of the devout. They ask how such an ordered universe could come into being. For the serious spiritual seeker, God may or may not exist, but there is something beyond reason, beyond the mind. As Shakespeare said, 'There are more things in heaven and earth, Horatio, than are dreamt of in your philosophy.' *Hamlet*. As for the violence and suffering caused by religion, they may say that things would have been far worse but for religion. Religion puts a brake on the evil tendencies of men. The usual retort is that many people do evil things in the name of religion. The other side then says that evil people are not religious; they misuse religion for personal ends.

There will always be a debate between the devout and the sceptic. The purpose here is neither to defend religion nor to take a position on God or the existence of any ultimate truth. The limited purpose is to see what the great sacred texts say. If there is some harmony among them, that in itself reveals something.

Structure of Religions

As stated earlier, the great religions begin with revelation. For instance, Moses saw a burning bush and heard the word of God and the Ten Commandments. Buddha sat under the banyan tree and got enlightened. Mohammad repeatedly heard the voice of Allah, revealed to him through the angel Gabriel. These are examples of revelation. Similar events are described in all the sacred texts.

A second aspect of a religion is the practice. The founders often provided practical ways of following their teachings. For instance, Buddha taught the Eight Fold Path, which is a set of practices for discovering the truth he preached. Sikhism extols the practice of feeding others. It is a religious practice. In Judaism, there are the Ten Commandments. The Bhagavad Gita contains practical teachings about how to live. The Quran gives instructions about how to behave and act, and to perform charity. Without exception, all religions have teachings about practical living based on morals, ethics and love.

A third aspect of religion is philosophy and metaphysics. This goes into questions about God, the universe and the ultimate destiny of the human being. For example, Buddhism has a rich literature with philosophies like *Shunya* and *Madhyamaka*. There are different sects like Theravada, Mahayana, Vajrayana, Zen and so on. Their texts are not the words of Buddha, and often, these philosophies differ among themselves. These later philosophies have a lower status than the words and teachings of the founders. They are considered products of the mind and reason and are not considered revelations. They go into great detail, interpret the teachings of the founders and sometimes establish new doctrines. Most were written centuries after the ancient, original texts. The essence of a religion, and a search for harmony, cannot be found in these later texts of various sects. Fortunately, all the great religions have one set of holy books that are considered the most sacred. We study these original holy books and see if there is any harmony among the various religions.

A fourth aspect is ritual. Rituals are tied up with the practice. For instance, in Hinduism, worship, meditation or contemplation is practised. This is often followed by a ritual offering of the results of the worship to God or a higher power. Here, it is difficult to separate the act from the ritual. But there are rituals in all religions about how worship is to be conducted—seated, kneeling, facing a particular direction, bathing, wearing certain types of dress and so on. There are rituals regarding dress, food and other elements of daily life.

Another important aspect is folklore and mythology. Stories about the origin of the world, floods, ancient

kings, miracles, prophets and Gods are told in every
religion. Even an atheistic religion like Jainism has
mythology, as does Buddhism, an agnostic religion. We
do not examine why there is mythology in every religion.
That requires a much more detailed and separate study.
How does a prophet explain her or his revelation to large
masses of people? Unlike a scholar, who seeks rigour
and addresses other scholars, the prophet or founder of
a religion addresses the whole of society. For instance,
Jesus is asked by his close followers, 'Why do you speak
to them in parables?' He replied, 'You have been given
the opportunity to know the secrets of the kingdom of
heaven, but they have not. For this reason, I speak to
them in parables: although they see, they do not see,
and although they hear, they do not hear, nor do they
understand.' (Gospel of Mathew 13:10, 13:11 and 13:13)
Without exception, the founders and prophets spoke to
the whole of society, often in stories, parables and using
everyday common examples. Written records were not
available and there was an oral tradition. It is difficult and
perhaps impossible to establish the historical accuracy of
ancient myths. Even today, we find people who believe
in apparently miraculous events, whether of ancient
times or of modern times. Whatever the reasons may be,
mythology is a strong element in all religions.

Thus, all religions have revelation, philosophy, practice,
ritual and mythology. All religions, without exception,

have various sects and each has its own philosophy. Such philosophical texts were written centuries after the founder passed away. Here, we do not examine these texts in detail. Fortunately, the sects and philosophies in each religion accept the supremacy of the original holy texts. Ritual and practice are also linked and it is not always easy to differentiate between them. For instance, there is worship in every religion. Even in Buddhism, the followers show great reverence to Buddha. Jainism, which is explicitly atheist, has temples with idols of ancient saints. Such worship can be considered a ritual. But in another sense, it is an essential practice. The forms of worship differ, but the inner thought, mood or emotion is very similar across religions. By practices here we mean the translation of the essential teachings into action. For instance, to cultivate feelings of compassion and love towards one's fellow beings is taught in all religions. We can translate that into action by prayer, by giving of alms, by the gifts of knowledge, by caring for those who suffer and so on. But modes of dress, the unique methods of worship (waving a lit lamp, kneeling or prostrating, facing a particular direction and so on), injunctions about what kinds of food are prohibited and allowed, the ways of conducting marriages and funerals are all rituals. We do not study them here. In fact, it is by observing rituals of other religions and by superficial hearsay about the founders and texts that we form fairly strong opinions about them.

The founders give some teachings about how to practise their religion. Their purpose was not to create an intellectual framework or philosophy. Their purpose was to help those around them to lead a better, happier and more meaningful life, and they knew that elaborate scholarly writings did not interest the general public. The founders rarely spoke of rituals. For instance, the Sikhs adopt a dress code. The founder, Guru Nanak, did not prescribe any such code. This was introduced centuries later by one of his followers, who was the tenth Guru.

In this book, we examine the initial revelations. We also examine the practices that lead to a better life. For instance, one practice or teaching is about love. Without exception, all religions have preached this. Hinduism says the world is your family, Buddha says live for the welfare and happiness of the many—*bahujana hitaya, bahujana sukhaya*, Christ says love thy neighbour as thyself. The teachings of the founders that are meant to be put into practice are also studied.

Revelation

The very foundation of religion is revelation. All the great religions stake their claim on the founders getting some kind of divine knowledge or extrasensory knowledge of a higher truth. 'Every great religion acknowledges revelation in the wide sense that its followers are dependent on the privileged insights of its founder or of the original group or individuals with which the faith began. These profound insights into the ultimate meaning of life and the universe, which have been handed down in religious traditions, are arrived at, it is believed, not so much through logical inference as through sudden, unexpected illuminations that invade and transform the human spirit.[1]

These were put down in the most sacred texts and form the basis of the religion. In the Abrahamic religions, the first was Judaism. God or Yahweh taught a series of prophets, starting with Abraham. Christianity and Islam also accept that these early prophets received such revelations. Such revelations were through voices, visions and sometimes miracles and dreams. Since some of the revelations included prophecies about future events and were proved right, faith in the religion grew. Christianity is based on Jesus Christ, an incarnation of God, who directly taught the word of God. Islam is based on the revelations that the Prophet Mohammad received over two decades from Allah through the angel Gabriel. In the Indian religions, Hinduism is based on the *shruti,* the revealed texts, which are the four Vedas and within that the Upanishads, also known as the Vedanta. These revelations were obtained by the rishis or seers of the Upanishads. Buddhism is based on the revelations of Buddha, and Jainism on the revelations of Mahavira and the earlier Tirthankaras or enlightened teachers.

Sikhism is based on the divine revelations of the founder, Guru Nanak.

It is therefore important to get a clear idea of what is meant by the word revelation. One view is that it is derived from the Greek word *apokalypsis,* which means removing the veil. The ultimate reality or truth is hidden, as it were, and revelation removes the veil covering it. There could be several veils covering the ultimate truth. Revelation is said to be intuitive, supersensory, revealing truths that were otherwise not known, a direct experience of something beyond the mundane or the world.

One important aspect of the revelation is that it transforms the individual who receives it. It is not like any other experience, thought or dream. People sense that something has changed in the individual who has received the revelation. He or she speaks words of wisdom, and is accepted as a teacher. Swami Vivekananda says such a person goes into the revelation a fool and comes out a sage.

Some examples may help to grasp this idea. In Hinduism, the unknown sage of the Rig Veda says, '*Vedahametam Purusha mahantam, aditya varnam, tamasah parastaat*', meaning 'I have seen that supreme Purusha, brilliant like the sun, beyond all darkness'. It clearly refers to some inner experience of the ultimate reality, here called Purusha, and elsewhere called Atman or Brahman. In The Gospel of John, 10:30, Jesus Christ says, 'I and the Father are One', meaning he is identical with God. Jesus is relating an inner experience. Though there is a separate book of revelations in the New Testament, here we limit the examples to the revelations of the founders. The Hadith describes changes in the Prophet Mohammad when he received a revelation. He would break into a cold sweat even on a cold day, see visions and hear voices or sounds like the ringing of a bell. In Hinduism, advanced yogis sometimes speak privately of the hearing of such sounds. Allah at such times spoke to the Prophet through the angel Gabriel. In Judaism, Moses saw a burning bush that was not consumed and heard the voice of God or Yahweh, who said in one instance, 'I am That I Am'. God was telling Moses to tell the people about who God is. Since there is no description possible, the phrase 'I am That I Am' is heard by Moses. The Japji in Sikhism is an inspired set of verses describing the ultimate reality. It starts off by saying that there is One name of Truth, doer and creator, fearless, without hatred, beyond time, yet manifest, unborn, self-existent. By the Guru's grace it can be realized. Later it says God is in Shiva, Gorak, Brahma, Mother Parvati (Hindu gods); he who possesses this knowledge cannot describe it in in words.

Even in the agnostic and atheist religions like Buddhism and Jainism, the basis is revelation, variously called wisdom, complete knowledge and so on, leading to nirvana or liberation from all worldly sorrows. Buddha says in the Udānavarga (Nirvāṇavarga 26–24, 25), 'That place where the elements are not found I know. There is neither space nor consciousness, no sun nor moon; no coming, no going, no rebirth, no passing away. It is without support or object—this is called the end of suffering.' Jainism refers to Kevala Jnana or complete knowledge as the state of the liberated person.

Mysticism is considered an essential aspect of revelation. This word has been used loosely and repeatedly and is understood vaguely. Evelyn Underhill says, 'One of the most abused words in the English language, it ("mysticism") has been used in different and often mutually exclusive senses by religion, poetry, and philosophy: has been claimed as an excuse for every kind of occultism, for dilute transcendentalism, vapid symbolism, religious or aesthetic sentimentality, and bad metaphysics. On the other hand, it has been freely employed as a term of contempt by those who have criticized these things. . . Broadly speaking, I understand it to be the expression of the innate tendency of the human spirit towards complete harmony with the transcendental order; whatever be the theological formula under which that order is understood. This tendency, in great mystics, gradually captures the whole field of consciousness; it dominates their life and, in the experience called "mystic union", attains its end . . . the desire to attain it and the movement towards it—so long as this is a genuine life process and not an intellectual speculation—is the proper subject of mysticism.'[2]

A rational view does not give importance to revelation. It is sometimes explained as imagination or even hallucination and self-delusion. Modern philosophical enquiry refers to the 'hard problem of consciousness'. Explained in various ways, it asks the question that after all rational explanations have been exhausted, why should there be any experience? Thus living beings experience the world, their thoughts, feelings of pain and pleasure and so on. Some thinkers reject the notion of consciousness and say experience is a product of biological processes in the nervous system and the brain. Even consciousness itself is a product of other physical processes. So we have two views: one is that consciousness is primary and fundamental and that physical phenomena and biological processes are perceived and experienced by this consciousness. For our purpose, this consciousness, at one level, 'experiences' revelation. The other view is that there is no fundamental 'thing' called consciousness. So revelation itself is an outcome of natural processes and phenomena. But there is no final conclusion. There is growing literature on this subject, but here we discuss what the great religions base themselves on—which is revelation.

Such a revelation is from God or truth or some higher source. Revelations could be about truth itself, some inner experience (in eastern religions called *samadhi*), about the world, about practical teachings, about right conduct, morals and ethics. In some cases they are about future events, about how to act and so on. Secondary literature has developed in all religions explaining the revelations and teachings. In some sacred texts, there is an invitation to everyone to follow the teachings, follow the disciplines and receive enlightenment and revelation. In other texts, the emphasis is on following the teachings and on moral and ethical conduct.

Even these revelations are given in the language, culture and customs of the society and times when the prophets and founders received them. For example, the angel Gabriel is the medium through which Allah revealed the truth to Prophet Mohammad. In eastern cultures, there is no concept of the angel Gabriel. To take another example, Buddha left home as a wandering monk in search of enlightenment even though he had everything—health, youth, a beautiful wife, a life of luxury and the right to inherit a kingdom. The tradition of monks leaving home and family and living on alms was common in India. It was not present in the Abrahamic religions except in Christianity. Buddha had to fight Mara, who first tempted him, then threatened him. But Buddha overcame all obstacles and became enlightened. Mara is the personification of forces like greed, ego, lust, hate, jealousy and so on that are obstacles to enlightenment. In the New Testament, we see Satan tempting Jesus Christ, offering him the kingdom of the world. He overcomes Satan using the famous words 'Get thee behind me, Satan'. Satan is the Middle Eastern version of Mara.

How is a revelation communicated to the general public in words? Some religions like Buddhism and Hinduism explicitly say that the ultimate reality cannot be described in words. Nevertheless, the statements of those who received such revelations are with us. The revelation, which is an inner experience, is converted to words and set in the context of the culture and society of those times. A proper study of the words in the sacred texts would require deeper contemplation of the meaning rather than a focus on the story, symbols and so on.

So the important question is: if all religions are based on revelation, where can we find them? They are available in the most sacred texts, which is why we need to study them before we search for any harmony or unity among religions.

The Sacred Texts

The founders taught the people around them, who took notes or memorized the teachings. It is believed that the teachings were based on the revelations received by the founder(s) or, in some cases, the very words of the founder were considered revelations.

How do we begin such a study of the sacred texts? There are two major regions where the great religions originated. Hinduism, Jainism, Buddhism and, much later, Sikhism came from India. Judaism, Christianity and Islam originated in the Middle East. Zoroastrianism, an ancient religion, came from Persia or modern-day Iran. There are many other religious traditions around the world, but either they do not stake their claim on revelation, or they do not have any written sacred texts. We do not study such religions in this book.

Without exception, the sacred texts of the great religions were compiled over decades or centuries. The canonical* versions were finalized decades or sometimes centuries after the founders had passed away. In the two oldest religions, Hinduism and Judaism, there were oral traditions that kept the teachings alive for centuries before they were put down in written form. For the devout and the orthodox, the words of the sacred canonized texts today are final. However, given the history of these sacred texts, it is impossible to know the exact words of the founders. Even within a religion with different versions of the sacred texts, the final authority of the founder or prophet, and the supremacy of the sacred texts, is accepted by all.

Hinduism, also known as the Sanatana Dharma or the eternal religion, has many sacred texts and no single

---

* Canonical: included in the list of sacred books officially accepted as genuine.

founder. The sages or rishis of the Vedic times received revelations, and so Hinduism is sometimes called the Vedic religion. Within the numerous sacred texts, the highest place is given to the Vedas, and within that to the later portion known as Vedanta or the Upanishads. These are called shruti or the revealed texts. We provide the essence of these texts. A widely accepted norm in Hinduism is the idea of the *prasthana traya*, or the first three sacred texts, which are the Vedas (which include the Upanishads), the Brahma Sutras and the Bhagavad Gita. The Brahma Sutras give a philosophy based on the revelations in the Upanishads. The Bhagavad Gita gives many practical teachings as well as revelations and philosophy.

The most sacred texts of Jainism came from Mahavira. He was the twenty-fourth and the last Tirthankara or fully enlightened teacher. Over the next few centuries, the religion gradually broke into two sects, the Digambara and the Svetambara. The teachings were orally transmitted from teacher to disciple for a few centuries. Apparently, due to prolonged famine, the number who had learnt the texts dwindled. The texts were then written down from memory. There were differences between the sects about the actual sacred texts. We will focus mainly on two that are accepted by both sects, namely the Tattvartha Sutra and a recent text called the Saman Suttam. However, there is common ground in the other texts, and we will use them to highlight the essential ideas in Jainism. In line with the theme of this book, we focus on the spiritual, moral and ethical teachings as well as the practices.

Buddhism was founded by Buddha. While the exact dates are not established, a popular scholarly view is that he lived for eighty years between 563 BCE and 483 BCE. He was born into a royal family, was married at sixteen and had one son. He renounced the world at the age of twenty-nine and left home in search of enlightenment. After six years of intense struggle, he attained Nirvana and became Buddha. He learnt from many teachers. But in the end, he decided to fall back on his own resources to find the truth. His first sermon, given in Sarnath near Banaras, is well known for expounding the Four Noble Truths. Most scholars agree that this is the basis of Buddha's entire teachings. His later sayings often included these Four Noble Truths.

There is a wealth of literature available on Buddhism. Buddhism also split into various sects. We, however, study the original words of Buddha in the Tripitakas or the three baskets of sacred texts. The Vinaya Pitaka is a compilation of rules for monks. The Sutta Pitaka has the direct teachings of Buddha, sometimes called Buddhavachana, and the third, the Abhidhamma Pitaka, is a scholarly and intellectual exposition of the teachings. In the spirit of this book, we largely study the Sutta Pitaka. These three texts are the most sacred for the Theravada school of Buddhism. However, there are other sects of Buddhism, like Mahayana and Vajrayana, who do not give the same position to the Tripitakas.

From the Middle East, the most ancient religion is Judaism. It is not based on a single founder but on the teachings of several prophets. A basic Jewish text is the Torah, which consists of the five books known as the Pentateuch. This contains all the aspects of religion discussed earlier, namely, the revelations, the teachings about what to do, philosophy, rituals and mythology. The Jewish people believe that God revealed the contents of the Torah to Moses. However, the texts were canonized much later, and some portions were deleted and a final version perhaps became available in the first century CE. Another important ancient text is the Nevi'im or Prophets, containing the lives and teachings of the ancient teachers who succeeded Moses. A third ancient book is the Ketuvim or Writings, sometimes known as the Hagiographa. They contain poetry, songs, wisdom and history. This was canonized much later. Together, they form the Jewish Bible, also called the Tanakh or Mikra. It is known by non-Jews as the Old Testament. One famous revelation is the one Moses received on Mount Sinai, now known as the Ten Commandments. Another later text of importance is the Talmud. One part of it is called the Oral Torah or Mishna, which was given long ago by Moses but was written down later. A second part of the Talmud is the Gemera, which is the work of later Jewish rabbis and gives an interpretation of the Oral Torah. For the purposes of this book, we go back to the written texts that are widely accepted as the foundational or original texts.

Christianity is the next great religion that came from the Middle East. Its founder was Jesus Christ, who was born a Jew. He lived for only thirty-three years, but a complete biography is not available. However, the last three years of his ministry are well-recorded. The Christians believe that Jesus was the Son of God and received many revelations. His teachings are given in the New Testament. The New Testament includes the Four Gospels of Mathew, Mark, Luke and John. The well-known Sermon on the Mount that Jesus preached is from the Gospel of Mathew. It also has the Letters, written by Paul, James, Peter, John and Jude, as well as the Revelations of John. Later, many other texts were written by various scholars and saints. In the spirit of this book, we focus our study on the Gospels as they contain the words of Jesus.

Islam is the last great religion that came from the Middle East. It was founded by the Prophet Mohammad. The most sacred book for the Muslims is the Quran. It is also considered by Muslims that God revealed the sacred words through the angel Gabriel to Prophet Mohammad, which were recorded and became the Quran. Another great text is the Hadith, which contains the recollections of various people who were close to the Prophet. It is widely believed that this had the tacit approval of Mohammad.

The Sunna is another sacred text that has many practices and rituals. Again, it is believed that this had the tacit approval of Mohammad. We largely focus on the Quran for the purposes of this text.

All the Abrahamic religions share a common set of prophets. Christianity accepts the prophets of the earlier Judaic religion. Islam also accepts the same set of prophets and also includes Jesus.

Another ancient religion is Zoroastrianism. It was founded by Zarathustra in what is today called Iran. The most sacred text is the Zendavesta. Accompanying this are the Pahlavi texts, which contain traditions, ceremonies, rituals and customs. Among the ancient religions with a written text, this has the least number of followers. Most of them fled to India after some invasions and are known as the Parsis, a prominent but small community.

In the late middle ages, the Sikh religion was founded by Guru Nanak in the state of Punjab in India. He travelled widely all over India and even went to Mecca and Medina. Since this is of recent origin, the life and teachings of the founder are available. The sacred text is known as the Guru Granth Sahib.

It is to be noted that in all the religions discussed so far, the original teachings were compiled after the passing away of the founder or prophets. These compilations were based on the recollections of those who were close to the founder. In Judaism, which does not have a single founder, the basic text, Torah, was compiled much after Moses passed away. In Hinduism, the Vedas and Upanishads, to which we refer in this book, were part of an oral tradition for centuries. The authors' or rishis' names are often not known. The texts were later put down in writing.

The religious impulse has been manifested in several other ways. There are indigenous and ethnic religions that exist in all parts of the world, some predating even the well-known religions mentioned here. Such religions are practised in South America, among the native Indians in the US and Canada, in Africa and in all parts of Asia, from the Middle East to China. The Far East has well-known religious teachers like Confucius and Lao Tzu in China, and indigenous religions like Shintoism in Japan. In Europe, there was paganism, with the Greek and Norse gods, as well as local practices and rituals. This was later replaced by Christianity. Even in India, rural religions involving various deities, symbols, rituals and ceremonies continue to exist. Sometimes, they are referred to as pagan or shamanistic where spirits are invoked. Some local customs and ceremonies persist in some regions, but many also follow one of the so-called mainstream religions. We do not discuss these religions as there are no written texts available today for most of them. The teachings of Confucius are available, but there are no claims to revelation. The teachings of Lao Tzu do refer to revelations, but there are very few followers who identify themselves as his followers. In this book, we do not discuss these religions.

Philosophy in Religion

The word philosophy has several connotations. Here, we refer to philosophy as applied to religion. All the religions have developed elaborate philosophies. For instance, Buddhism has the philosophies of Shunya (loosely translated as nothingness) and Madhyamaka. Christian philosophy tends to use the word Theology, referring to the study of God and religious belief. Several scholars and saints emerged, like St Thomas of Aquinas, who developed natural theology, St Ignatius Loyola, who founded the Society of Jesus, and others. Hinduism developed a whole range of philosophies, including the Six Philosophies known as the Shat Darsanas, and centuries later, the Advaita, Visishtadvaita and Dvaita philosophies.

All these philosophies came later and were not propagated by the founders. For instance, the Christian concept of the Holy Trinity of God, Jesus and the Holy Spirit is mentioned only in passing in the Gospels as the words of Jesus Christ. Similarly, the elaborate discussions in the Buddhist Madhyamaka philosophy are not found in the teachings of Buddha. The detailed philosophical treatises in Hinduism are not mentioned in the Vedas and Upanishads, the holiest of texts. These philosophies are based on reason and come from the mind. They are not based on revelation. One philosophy often differs from another even within the same religion. They arose for a variety of reasons. Later scholars and saints in a religion had to explain the original texts and revelations to the general public as well as to more rational and educated people. Often, they had to do this when other religions had become prevalent in the same geographic region. To establish their own religion more firmly, scholarly studies and writings perhaps became necessary.

In this book, we do not examine these philosophies. They are far more voluminous than the original sacred texts. They are of interest to the serious student and to scholars. Their influence on the practice of religion is at best indirect. In any case, all these philosophies defer to the holiest texts. The writers of these philosophies never claimed that they were equal to the founders. Most did not claim that they had obtained any revelation. In some cases, the philosophers were also mystics. But their philosophies did not in any way contradict the original texts.

Mythology

No religion is without mythology. There are stories and poems about the origin of the world, about creation, about miracles, fantastic deeds and events, floods that destroyed the earth, about saints, demons, angels, heroes, wars, kings, empires and so on. The myth of a huge flood that almost destroyed the earth is there in the Abrahamic religions and in Hinduism. There are stories about angels in the Abrahamic religions and about Devas, the shining ones and gods of rain, fire and so on in Hinduism. Even Buddhism has several references to miracles performed by Buddha, and to supernatural beings who came to listen to his teachings.

Mythology is another area of modern research. One fundamental question is: why was there a need to create mythology? Rationalists say the time for mythology is long over and that they should be abandoned. Other scholars like C.G. Jung and J. Campbell argue that myths embody a deeper psychological or subliminal truth that helps people and keeps the religion intact. For instance, in the Bhagavata Purana of Hinduism, there are stories of Krishna as a baby, a child and a young boy performing many miracles—showing the whole universe in his mouth, killing a demoness by suckling her breasts, killing a huge poisonous snake, holding up an entire hill on his small finger to save the people from a deluge and so on. Some Hindus (though not all) see Krishna as a lovable, all-powerful god who protects them. The philosophy of Krishna in another text, the Bhagavad Gita, is not fully known to many Hindus and they cannot relate to the Krishna of the Gita in the same intimate way as they can to the child Krishna of the Bhagavata Purana.

In Judaism, the Ten Commandments were accepted by many back then because God spoke these words to Moses, who then wrote it on a tablet for posterity. The Commandments by themselves are acceptable, but the appeal increases because Moses heard it directly from God. Another myth is of God creating the world in six days and taking rest on the seventh. So one day in the week became the day of rest. This was accepted widely because God Himself rested on that day. The many miracles that Moses performed even before fleeing Egypt shows that Yahweh, the One God, is more powerful than the polytheistic gods of the Egyptians and the Egyptian King, Pharaoh. The miracles helped the Jews leave Egypt when the king wanted to keep them enslaved. When the Egyptians later pursued them, Moses parted the Red Sea on God's command and the Semites escaped, while the pursuing Egyptians perished in the waters as they rolled back. This story increases faith among the followers that God is with them, that God is all-powerful and that Moses is a prophet. So they listened to him and followed him. When they did not, they suffered.

Even an agnostic, rational religion like Buddhism has myths. The Jataka tales of the 500 previous lives of Buddha say that sometimes he was born as an animal, sometimes as a man. The essence of all the stories is that Buddha was always truthful, compassionate, wise and strove to do good to everyone. These stories reinforce the values of truth, compassion and selflessness. Later, when he became Buddha, even the heavenly angels and gods came to learn from him. Sometimes they challenged him, but by his spiritual power he overcame their jealousy and they became his disciples. He subdues the fierce, evil murderer, Angulimala, who had a garland of finger bones from each of the people he had killed. Buddha subdues him without raising his hands or using a weapon. His spiritual power is sufficient to convert him, and Angulimala falls at Buddha's feet. This reinforces faith among the followers that Buddha was indeed great, nay, the greatest, greater even than the gods. So we must follow his teachings.

Jesus Christ also performed many well-known miracles—walking on water, making wine from water, feeding the crowds with a loaf of bread, making the lame walk, raising the dead and purifying prostitutes. A central miracle is that of resurrection when Jesus comes back from the dead after crucifixion and is seen by his close disciples. This serves to increase people's faith in Jesus as the Saviour.

The Prophet Mohammad had a vivid vision or dream where he was taken on a winged horse up to heaven and came very close to Allah. He leaves from Mecca, and on the way, he gets down and prays at Jerusalem. From there, he ascends on the shining winged horse to the seventh heaven. On the way, he passes the earlier prophets one by one, including Adam, Jesus, Joseph, Enoch, Aaron, Moses and Abraham. This serves to increase the faith of the devout that there is God, that Mohammad is indeed a prophet and actually saw God. For the ardent, the Prophet Mohammad may have exceeded the earlier prophets in holiness as he passed them in lower levels of heaven and came into proximity with God. This faith helps them follow all the other teachings and tenets of Islam.

Try as we may, mythology is not going to disappear from religion. The agnostics and atheists point to the myths to explain why they do not believe in God or religion. They say there are vested interests—priests, evangelists and gurus—who use these myths to create a large following for material benefit without imparting any real benefit. Among the religious, there are those who are more rational and do not completely believe the myths. But they, along with the more devout, get the essential underlying message of the myth—that God will help us, protect us and even lead us from darkness to light if we follow the teachings. There are others who want to see 'signs' and miracles before they believe anything about a prophet or religion. If they believe the myths, then they believe in the religion. Even among the non-believers, there is a significant group, which considers these mythological stories an important aspect of the culture they have been born into.

In this book, we do not discuss mythology and miracles in detail. In a later chapter, we examine some common elements of religious mythology across religions. Myths serve to reinforce faith but are not the essence of a religion.

Outside religion, there are folktales, parables, fairy tales and so on in all regions of the world. Since they have nothing much to do with God or religion, these tales are interesting by themselves. They often have a symbolic significance and imbue the culture with meaning.[3]

Practical Teachings

Religion also tells us what to do, and equally importantly, what not to do. Different teachings are picked up by different individuals based on what they seek from religion. For instance, Sikhism says '*naam japo, kirat karo, vand chhako*', meaning repeat the name of God (or always remember God), work honestly and share your wealth with everyone. These are simple, practical teachings that anyone can understand. These teachings are conveyed in different words in other religions as well. To love and remember God and pray to Him is a practice in all theistic religions. The value of honesty and avoiding laziness is emphasized in all religions. It is there in the Ten Commandments, in the Quran, in the Yoga sutras of Hinduism, which say we should avoid stealing, in the Bhagavad Gita, which says avoid inaction and work intelligently. To share with others is also taught in all religions. Love thy neighbour as thyself is a well-known teaching of Jesus, as is the idea of '*atithi devo bhava*', meaning the guest is god, in Hinduism, and the Quranic injunction to share food with those around you. These kinds of teachings attract followers and are more universal.

But there are other teachings too. As mentioned earlier, Jesus spoke to his close disciples about the secrets of the Kingdom of God, but in parables to the general people. He explains this by saying, 'Although they see, they do not see, and although they hear, they do not hear, nor do they understand.' (Mathew 13.13) In another instance, Jesus tells a rich, young man to sell everything he has, give to the poor and follow him. This is a direct teaching. When the young man is unable to do that, Jesus says it is easier for a camel to pass through the eye of a needle than for a rich man to enter the gates of heaven. These teachings are not for everyone, only for the chosen few who care for nothing but God. Even in Buddhism, there are separate teachings for householders and for monks—rather, for those who want to enjoy the world here and now, and for those are done with worldly enjoyment and seek Nirvana.

Thus, there are different levels of teachings. There are moral and ethical teachings. There are exhortations to be charitable. There are teachings about controlling our own mind—avoiding negative emotions like hatred, jealousy, greed, unrestrained lust, anger, laziness, egotistical behaviour and cultivating positive emotions like compassion, love, friendliness, peace and so on. This is common across all religions, whether theistic, agnostic (Buddhism) or atheistic (Jainism). For those who are more serious, there are teachings about how to reach the Kingdom of God, Nirvana and beatitude. Such practical teachings are discussed in later chapters within each religion. Later, some common teachings across religions are also discussed.

Rituals

Rituals are an important aspect of religion. In fact, there are rituals separate from religion as well. Social and business conventions about dress, about how to address others, what to say, what not to say and even how to eat are prevalent in all societies. For instance, in earlier days, business meetings required people to wear a particular dress (e.g., in western societies men wore a dark suit and a tie). In certain formal settings, one is not supposed to eat with one's hands, whereas in traditional Hindu weddings and feasts, one is expected to eat with the hands. Many organized societies and organizations have rituals, even if they are not religious. The armed forces in all countries have a clearly defined set of rituals—how to dress, how to address seniors, how to salute and so on. In eastern cultures, especially Japan, Korea and China, some rituals dictate how people interact with each other, how to greet seniors, how to speak, when to speak and so on. The Olympic Games open with a grand ritual, as do many modern games. Sometimes they sing the national anthem. Even in sports, it is common to see some great players perform a small, personal ritual before they start playing. It could be bouncing a ball a few times, touching the nose, rearranging one's hair, adjusting a cap or dress and so on. A player goes through the same set of actions or rituals before play starts after a break.

Religion also has rituals. They relate to worship, which itself has an elaborate set of rituals in some religions, including days of fasting or feasting, chanting sacred texts, avoiding certain foods and eating other kinds of food, as well as dress, the way of styling one's hair and so on. All religions use symbols, even if some of them prohibit images and idols.

Rituals help some people to structure their work and actions. For instance, in Hinduism, before meditation, the individual goes ideally to a calm and quiet place, lights some incense if possible, sits in a particular way, breathes slowly to calm the mind and then begins meditation according to instructions he or she may have received. Others may not like meditation. They may like group worship or singing. They learn some religious songs and sing in a group. Some ritual worship may be conducted by a priest. Even in Buddhism, there are references to rituals. For instance, in the Sutra Pitaka, there are many references to people who come to learn from Buddha. They bow to him, go around him, keeping him always to the right (i.e., in a clockwise direction) and then sit down at a lower level than his. Buddha then gives the teaching.

It is likely that the prophets and founders knew that different people needed different teachings. So sometimes we see them criticizing rituals. Jesus says, 'The Sabbath was made for man, not man for the Sabbath.' (Mark 2:27) Elsewhere, he tells us to shut the door and pray in secret, and that God will reward those who do so in secret. Jesus is doing away with rituals. But he also says, 'Think not that I am come to destroy the law, or the prophets: I am not come to destroy, but to fulfil the law' (Mathew 5:17). He is referring to the Old Testament, which has many rituals. Buddha never tells those who bow down to him and respectfully go around him not to do so. Hindu texts are numerous. The Upanishads do away with all rituals, whereas the Agama Sastras and some portions of the Vedas give detailed instructions on how to conduct ritual worship. The Torah is full of exhortations on some rituals, including the way worship is to be conducted in the tabernacle.

Rituals are numerous, vary within a religion from region to region, are different for men and women and vary for an individual as he or she moves from childhood to adolescence, adulthood and old age. We not do not study the rituals in religion. It is to be noted that for certain devout or even serious spiritual seekers, rituals help them practise religion.

Organization of the Sacred Texts

Some religious texts have kept revelations, philosophy, practice, mythology and rituals separate. For instance, in

Hinduism, the revelations are largely in the Upanishads; the Bhagavad Gita also has revelations but they are reported by the author. The philosophies are in the Shat Darsanas or Six Philosophies, and later in the Advaita, Visishtadvaita and Dvaita texts. Mythology is found largely in the Puranas, another set of eighteen texts. Rituals are described in the Karma Kanda or earlier sections of the Vedas as well as in the later Agama Sastras. Practical teachings are scattered across various texts, particularly in the Bhagavad Gita, in the Puranas and even in the Smritis.

However, in Judaism, the sacred texts are not separated in this manner. The most ancient and sacred set of texts found in the Torah, with its five books—Genesis, Exodus, Leviticus, Numbers and Deuteronomy—are arranged historically. All aspects of religion, from revelation, to philosophy, mythology, practice and ritual, are found in these texts. The Nevi'im or Prophets is largely historical and mythological. The Ketuvim contains songs, poems and wise sayings. This is true of Islam as well, where the Quran is the most sacred and contains all aspects of religion.

We provide a brief overview of the sacred texts of all religions. However, the focus of the discussion is on revelations and practices, which include moral and ethical teachings. As mentioned earlier, the mythologies differ, as do the rituals. Philosophy or theology in religion is also not discussed in detail as each religion has several sects with different philosophical texts. These texts were not written by the founders but by later scholars and saints. They do not have the same status as the founder or the most sacred texts.

We discuss the Abrahamic religions, Judaism, Christianity and Islam, followed by a discussion of the common essential aspects of these religions and where they differ as well. This is followed by the religions from India, Hinduism, Jainism, Buddhism and Sikhism. The common aspects of these religions are also discussed. We conclude by discussing all the religions.

THE ABRAHAMIC RELIGIONS

JUDAISM, CHRISTIANITY AND ISLAM

INTRODUCTION TO THE ABRAHAMIC RELIGIONS

Judaism, Christianity and Islam are known as the Abrahamic religions. They all trace their origin to the Prophet Abraham. Judaism is the oldest of the three and is dated approximately 1500 BCE. Christianity arose in the first century CE and Islam in the seventh century CE. Judaism and Christianity arose in the region around Jerusalem. Islam arose in Mecca, which is about 1,500 km away. Judaism was not influenced by the Indian religions, the most ancient of which, Hinduism, is dated a few centuries before that. Christianity originated in a Jewish region dominated by the rabbis or priests. Judaism preached monotheism and forbade idol worship, which was a prominent feature of the pre-existing religions of that region.

Christianity did not have to explicitly forbid it as by the time of Jesus Christ, idol worship did not exist in the region of Judea, of which Jerusalem was the central urban settlement. Islam, on the other hand, originated in Mecca, where idol worship was prevalent. Islam also forbids idol worship or image worship in any form.

All the three religions faced persecution. The Jews were enslaved and had to flee Egypt and fight to claim Israel. Christianity also faced persecution and Jesus was crucified. Most of his intimate disciples, or apostles, were also apparently killed. The Prophet Mohammad also faced persecution and had to flee to Yathrib, now known as Medina. People in the region knew of the two pre-existing religions, Christianity and Islam, which were known as the religions with a *kitab* or book.

All the three religions share the same belief in monotheism and they all forbid idol worship. They also share the same prophets. Christianity added Jesus and said he was the Son of God, but accepted the Old Testament or Torah and all the prophets there. Jesus said, "Do not think that I have come to abolish the Law or the Prophets; I have not come to abolish them but to fulfil them."(Mathew 5.17) Islam also accepts all the previous prophets of the Old Testament and Jesus. However, Islam does not accept Jesus as a Son of God, but as a prophet.

Judaism is a non-proselytizing religion, and does not convert anyone. In the twenty-first century, Christianity has the largest number of followers in the world, and Islam has the second largest. Both are proselytizing religions. All the religions ask their followers to follow the teachings of the scriptures. All three split over time into various sects. There is a mainstream religion, but there are also mystical offshoots of each religion. Jerusalem continues to be the most sacred city for Jews and Christians, and one of the most sacred for Islam. Mecca is the most sacred place for Muslims, followed by Medina. In modern times, there is greater contact and awareness among the religions of the world.

1

JUDAISM

Introduction

The sacred texts of Judaism are interwoven with all aspects of the religion—revelation, philosophy, mythology, practical teachings and rituals. Thus, there are references to what God said (revelation), philosophy about the role of humans, their relation with God, myths about creation, Noah's Ark, the parting of the Red Sea and the history of the prophets and the early followers. There are practical teachings about how to live, how to relate to God, family and others, even teachings about law and references to rituals about worship. It is therefore difficult to separate the different aspects of the religion in these texts.

This is unlike, say, Buddhism, where these aspects are dealt with either in separate texts or in separate sections of the same text. For instance, Buddha's words and teachings, considered revelation, are in the Sutta Pitaka, the philosophy in the Abhidhamma Pitaka and mythology like the Jataka tales in a separate section of the Sutta Pitaka. Such a broad separation of the different aspects of the religion is found in Hinduism as well. The different aspects are not in completely separate, watertight texts, but there is a clear emphasis on one or the other aspect.

In Judaism, the sacred texts in the Old Testament follow a historical timeline, beginning from creation and going on to Noah's Ark, the earliest prophets, including Abraham, Moses and the later prophets. Each of the five texts in the Old Testament mention all aspects of the religion. Judaism was the oldest religion in that part of the world. It arose among semi-nomadic tribes. Life was harsh by modern standards and water for settled agriculture was limited in the semi-arid region. Even Abraham first migrated several thousand kilometres to reach Canaan or modern-day Israel, then went further east to Egypt and then returned to Israel. There is a clear reference to migration from the promised land of Israel to Egypt due to drought, and in fact, Moses was born in Egypt among people who were enslaved.

To present God's teachings in such a context to the masses of people who were already used to polytheism, with multiple gods, idol worship and animal sacrifice, was perhaps a challenge for the prophets. Stories, myths and miracles performed by prophets formed an important part of the texts. God is presented as a powerful Being who requires complete obedience to his commands, who rewards those who follow them and occasionally punishes those who do not. Idol worship and polytheism are strictly prohibited, but animal sacrifice is not banned—it is now offered to a monotheistic God. So some aspects of the pre-existing polytheistic religions in that region were rejected and others accepted.

In contrast, early Hinduism, which slightly predates Judaism, originated in a relatively better climate with settled agriculture and a class of educated people. It started out without any idol worship described in the Vedas and Upanishads, which are the earliest and most sacred texts, and focused on revelation and philosophy. No doubt there were Vedic gods of rain, fire and so on, but they had no images or idols and God was formless. However, such minor gods were subsumed in the One Supreme Brahman or Reality. The core revelations of Hinduism, which are in the Upanishads or Vedanta, are completely devoid of image or idol worship. When the ideas spread a few centuries later to the masses, they were accompanied by myths, legends and miracles, along with idol worship and the acceptance of the idea that a formless God could have form as well.

In a sense, Judaism took the people away from idol worship to monotheism, while Hinduism took people from a formless God to idol worship. The reason seems to be the historical context.

Historical Context

Even a casual reading of the sacred texts shows some unique aspects of Judaism. There are repeated references to the promised land, what is now called Israel, and the promise that God made to Abraham, the first prophet, as well as to other prophets like Moses, to restore the land to them. It was also known then as Canaan and included modern-day Israel and parts of Lebanon. It is also referred to as the land of 'milk and honey' in the Old Testament. A later prophet, Jacob was also known as Israel, and his descendants and followers became known as Israelites. There is a 'covenant' or agreement between the people and God. In simple terms, God would fulfil His promises if the people followed his commands. There are references to long periods of enslavement of the Jews, liberation from the pharaohs of Egypt, wars, wanderings in the wilderness of the Sinai desert and great suffering and travails. There is a focus on a geographical region, on the people who have a covenant with God. There is a yearning, as it were, for the land of Israel as the sacred land.

Why do these concepts play such a prominent role in the sacred texts? It is important to understand the context of the time when Judaism first arose. There were several tribes, and sometimes there were conflicts between them. People worshipped idols and polytheism was prevalent. Many were semi-nomadic, though in some cases there was farming where water was available. Pre-existing rites, rituals, tribal laws and customs were prevalent.

Abraham lived in Ur Kasdim near modern-day Baghdad in Iraq. He led his people on a long migration to Canaan. The scriptures say that God told Abraham to settle down there, and that He would give this land to his descendants. Apparently, they practised polytheism earlier, but God commanded Abraham to adopt monotheism. Abraham, his son Isaac and his grandson Jacob lived in Canaan. Jacob was also called Israel. Due to natural disasters like drought, Jacob and his people migrated to Egypt. Here, they were subjugated and enslaved and were known as Israelites, the descendants of Israel or Jacob. They spoke what are now called Semitic languages, including Hebrew, which was distinct from the local language in Egypt. The dictionary defines semitic as 'of, relating to, or constituting a subfamily of the Afro-Asiatic language family that includes Hebrew, Aramaic, Arabic, and Amharic.' (Merriam-Webster Dictionary) Today, semitic is identified with Jews and antisemitism with being against the Jewish race. Scholars have studied the races that lived back then and there is no agreement except that the Israelites and Egyptians were most likely distinct races. In the Judaic sacred texts, Israel came to be identified with the original homeland from which the tribes had come. The Egyptians practised polytheism, while the Israelites believed in the One God.

According to the sacred texts, God had promised to give Israel back to the tribes descendant from Jacob. Moses was instrumental in fulfilling this promise. He was born in Egypt and was a fourth generation descendant of Jacob. He led his people out of Egypt and after forty years of wandering in the wilderness in the Sinai desert, brought them close to Canaan and died. His anointed successor, Joshua, led the people, who waged war and won Israel. This was the promised land. Banishment, enslavement, suffering and wandering intensified the longing for the promised land. God's covenant meant that if the people followed His teachings and commands, God would fulfil His promise. Whenever they did not, God would punish them. The forty years of wandering in the desert sometimes made people question Moses. This was also said to be a violation of God's commandments and a lack of faith. When people suffered due to war, natural calamities and enslavement, it was attributed to people not following God's commandments.

A large part of the sacred texts is centred on the life of Moses, perhaps the most prominent of the Judaic prophets. He spent most of his life in exile, away from Israel, in the wilderness. There is repeated reference to the promised land that God had said He would give them. This idea of a sacred land or location is found in all religions. The devout go on a pilgrimage to sacred places. However, the Israelites had to suffer in slavery and exile and fight to win back the sacred land. In other religions, people simply went on a pilgrimage to the holy lands and there was no strife.

Judaism originated in the Near East in Asia on the border between what is now Africa and Asia. There is no one founder and the earliest prophet was Abraham. The term 'Abrahamic religions' refers to Judaism, Christianity and Islam, which often refer to Abraham. He got a command from God to go forth into a new land. His faith in God is complete, and at one time, he is commanded to sacrifice his son Isaac. As he is about to do so, he is told that sacrificing a ram instead was good enough. The story emphasizes his complete faith and surrender to God's commands.

In the thirteenth or fourteenth century BCE, Moses received revelations on Mount Sinai from God. It has not been possible to locate exactly where Mount Sinai is, but in modern times, it is widely accepted to be in Egypt in the Sinai Peninsula. Mount Sinai is considered to be a sacred location in all the three Abrahamic religions. Today, Egypt is largely Islamic, but St Catherine's monastery has been there since the sixth century CE. A century or more later, the Prophet Mohammad gave a letter of protection to this monastery, and it still exists.

In the earlier traditions, God's name was not uttered as it was too sacred a word. In Hebrew, the word is Yahweh, and is usually translated as 'I am who I am' or 'I am that I am'. God is thus formless and all idol worship is prohibited. In those times, there were local traditions and customs which worshipped stone and other idols. But Judaism (and later Christianity and Islam) forbade it. There is only one God in monotheism.[*]

The Sacred Texts

The most sacred text is the Torah. Two other sacred texts are the Nevi'im or Prophets and the Ketuvim. These three together are called the Tanakh or Mikra. In English, this is the Hebrew Bible or the Old Testament. The Nevi'im has the lives and teachings of the prophets. The Ketuvim is sometimes known as the Hagiographa. It has poetry, songs, wisdom and history. Like some other religions, the texts were written down and accepted as final many centuries after Moses.

The Nevi'im contains the history of the prophets that came after Moses. The first set of books is about the earlier prophets, Joshua, Judges, Samuel and Kings. The second set is about the later prophets and has the books of Isaiah, Jeremiah, Ezekiel and twelve Minor Prophets. Joshua succeeded Moses and led the Jews into Israel. The prophets communicated with God, but were not portrayed as perfect. Many of their teachings, sayings and actions are

---

[*] A doctrine that says there is only one God

given in these texts. Much of it is of historical interest and not related to direct teachings from God.

The Ketuvim or Writings is divided into four sections. They are dated from the sixth century BCE to the second century CE. The poetical books are Psalms, Proverbs and Job. The Megillot has the Song of Solomon, Book of Ruth, Lamentations of Jeremiah, the Ecclesiastes and the Book of Esther. The third section is the Prophecy and the final one is History. We get a flavour of the contents from some of the sayings. One such is 'I (Yahweh) have said, *Ye are gods; and all of you are children of the most High*' from Psalm 82:6. This is a significant statement—that man is made in the image of God. Genesis 1:27 says 'So God created Man in His own image, in the image of God created He him; male and female he created.'

The Torah is given the highest place in Judaism. It consists of five books called the Law or Pentateuch by Christians. These are Genesis, Exodus, Leviticus, Numbers and Deuteronomy. It contains the well-known Ten Commandments. God revealed the truth to Moses and this was recorded in the Torah. Although these revelations were from the thirteenth or fourteenth century BCE, they were recorded and written down several centuries later. One estimate puts the dates as around the sixth century BCE while other estimates date it later. The teachings were presumably handed down over the centuries by oral tradition. Some parts that were not written down then continued and were referred to as the oral Torah.*

God commands Moses to go and teach the people. Moses asks God, 'Who shall I say has sent me to the people?' God said: 'I am that I am. Say that I am has sent you.'

The first book in the Torah is Genesis, or Bereshit in Hebrew. It talks about the genesis or beginning of everything. It says that God created the earth in six days and took rest on the seventh. God created the earth, waters, heavens, Sun, Moon, stars, plants and animals. He said, 'Let there be light' and there was day and night. He also created Man—both males and females—in His image.

It goes on to describe the creation of the wonderful garden of Eden and the story of Adam and Eve, the story of temptation and the expulsion of Adam and Eve from the Garden of Eden. It says that Cain killed his brother Abel and was banished by God. A lineage of the descendants is given. God is not happy with the evil deeds of the people. He decides to destroy mankind through a great flood and save only one pair from each species. The story of Noah's

---

* This is similar to the Vedas of Hinduism and the Jain scriptures which were recorded in writing centuries later. In the case of Buddhism it is said that the teachings of Buddha were recorded for the first time by his direct disciples a few decades after his passing away. The Christian Gospels were written down between 50 CE and 100 CE after the passing away of Jesus Christ

Ark is told, where two specimens of all living beings are taken aboard the Ark and survive the great flood. There are similar legends and myths of a great flood in Hinduism, in Greek mythology and in Mesopotamia.

Genesis then describes the descendants of Noah's Ark until it comes to Abraham. His life is described in some detail. In one significant incident, Abraham is asked by God to sacrifice his son. He is ready to do so, and just as he raises his knife, a voice calls out and tells him to stop. He is asked to sacrifice a ram (male sheep) instead. God is very pleased that Abraham unhesitatingly follows His commands.

Genesis continues to list the lineage of Abraham. His son Isaac continued the lineage. Jacob was Isaac's son and was renamed Israel. This is also the name of the country that is said to be the home of the Jews. Jacob's favourite son is Joseph, who is exiled to Egypt by his jealous brothers. He is jailed, but wins the pharaoh's favour by correctly interpreting his dreams. He rises in Egyptian society and saves it from famine. Later, Jacob's family also travels to Egypt to escape the famine. Jacob helps them settle in the Nile delta. Genesis ends with the death of Joseph, the favourite son of Jacob. Joseph wants his body to be removed from Egypt. This wish is fulfilled later by Moses when he flees Egypt in the next book, Exodus.

The next book is Exodus or Shemot in Hebrew. It begins with the birth of Moses. He was abandoned by his mother and adopted by the pharaoh's (king's) daughter. Later, the king wanted to kill Moses. So he fled Egypt and lived in the desert.

He then obtained the famous revelation on Mount Sinai. An angel led him to a bush 'that burned with fire, but was not consumed' (Exodus 3:2). When he went to see why the bush was not burnt, God called to him and said, 'Moses, Moses, Here I am' (Exodus 3:4). He is asked to remove his shoes as the ground under his feet is holy. God told him he was the God of his fathers—of Abraham, Isaac and Jacob. Moses hid his face as he was afraid to look. God told him that he would protect him and his people. Moses is told to go and gather the Hebrews in Egypt and bring them out of the country after taking the pharaoh's permission.

Moses is bewildered and asks who he should say has sent him. God said, 'I am that I am. Say to the children of Israel* than I Am has sent you.' God gives him the power to change a rod into a serpent and then back to a rod, and to cure leprosy. Moses later uses this to convince everyone that he is indeed a prophet. God promises him that he will guide him throughout and that Moses should take the help of his brother Aaron.

---

* Jacob, a prophet more ancient than Moses and grandson of Abraham, was later known as Israel. All who came after were then known as the children of Israel.

Through a series of miracles, Moses and Aaron bring about disasters in Egypt and convince the king that he should let the children of Israel leave Egypt. As they leave, God tells Moses to part the sea (now said to be the Red Sea). The Israelites cross the sea. The Egyptians who pursued them, however, perished in the waters as they rolled back.

The people undergo several hardships in the desert and there are murmurs of protest against Moses. God intervenes and provides them food and water. After forty years in the desert, God once again reveals Himself to Moses. He now gives several teachings. The best known of these are what are now called the Ten Commandments. They were accompanied by thunder, lightning, trumpeting and smoke. The people were afraid and stayed away from Mount Sinai and accepted Moses as their leader. Since they are so important, they are given below.

The Ten Commandments

1. I am the Lord thy God.
2. Thou shalt have no other gods before Me; Thou shalt not make a graven image; Thou shalt not bow down to any image or idol.
3. Thou shalt not take the name of the Lord thy God in vain.
4. Remember the sabbath day, to keep it holy. Six days shalt thou labour, and do all thy work; but the seventh day is a sabbath for God, you shall do no work.

5. Honour thy father and thy mother.
6. Thou shalt not kill.
7. Thou shalt not commit adultery.
8. Thou shalt not steal.
9. Thou shalt not bear false witness against thy neighbour.
10. Thou shalt not covet thy neighbour's house or wife.

Most of the teachings (seven) are about what should not be done. There are only two explicit 'dos'—keeping the day of sabbath holy and honouring one's father and mother. The first commandment is simply a statement of fact. The Ten Commandments are followed by teachings about family, children, servants and slaves. There are teachings about justice and punishment. There are detailed instructions about worship. A tabernacle (the earliest house of worship in Judaism) is constructed. But Moses could not enter it because there was a cloud of God that engulfed the tabernacle. Exodus ends saying that God guided the Israelites as they continued their journey by entering the tabernacle as a cloud by day and as fire by night.

The third Book is Leviticus or Vayikra in Hebrew. Vayikra refers to God calling out to Moses and giving him detailed instructions. Leviticus in Latin refers to the tribe of Levi, who were a priestly class. Moses and his brother Aaron belonged to this tribe. The book is meant for priests and has instructions about how worship is to be conducted. There are references to how animals are to be offered at the altar. For regular offerings, male animals are used, and for offerings to atone for sins, female. Animals that are forbidden to be eaten are named. Adultery of various forms is prohibited. Detailed instructions are given about how to worship and about the punishment for committing sins. Leviticus ends by saying that these are the teachings that God gave to Moses on Mount Sinai.

The fourth Book is Numbers or Bamidbar in Hebrew. God had promised Moses that his people will reach the Promised Land of Israel (also referred to as the land across the Jordan river, and as Canaan). God tells Moses to number the people who can bear arms, all the men who are above twenty years of age and found fit for military service. Over 6,00,000 are found to be fit. The Levites or priestly class were exempt from military service. They were dedicated to worship at the tabernacle, the earliest place of worship. As they set out from Sinai, they face many difficulties. The people murmur against Moses and God and are punished by God. Spies are sent to Canaan. They come back and report that the land is full of 'milk and honey'. They also say that the land is inhabited by giants. The people refuse to take arms as they were afraid.

They are condemned to wander in the wilderness. Many perish in the plague, which is seen as a punishment for disobeying God. People complain of the lack of water. God tells Moses to speak to a rock. When he initially disobeys, God tells him that he will not enter the land of

Canaan. This later turns out to be correct as Moses dies before the Israelites enter Canaan.

His sister Miriam and brother Aaron die. The Israelites intermarry with the local people and adopt some of their customs, including worshipping of their deities. This meant that they had not followed the commandment against idol worship. God sends a plague and many die. Moses again forbids worship of other gods.

Another census is taken, which also shows over 600,000 able-bodied males ready for war. Rules are made for how land is to be distributed in Israel once it is conquered.

It describes the tribes of the people who followed Moses. It gives the names of the elders of each. They were prepared for war.* Only the tribe of Levites were forbidden from war. These were the priests. A significant statement from God to Moses is 'Hear now my words. If there be a Prophet among you, I the Lord will make myself known unto him in a vision and will speak unto him in a dream' (12:6).† An important aspect of Moses's character is revealed here. First, when he is told that others in his following are also making prophecies, he does not become jealous, but says, 'Would God that all the Lord's people were prophets, and that the Lord would put his spirit upon

---

* This is somewhat similar to the descriptions in the Mahabharata of the various leaders or Kings who were getting ready for war.

† This is the same idea in all religions where God reveals deeper truths to prophets, saints and sages

22

them' (11:29). When Miriam, his sister, also considered a prophetess, is struck with leprosy, Moses prays for her recovery. The preparations for the war with Canaan (now part of modern-day Israel, and also centred on Palestine) begin. The followers of Moses are struck with fear at seeing the opposing forces. They want to go back to Egypt, and feel they were wrong in having followed Moses and living in the wilderness and wandering in the desert. God knows all this and wants to punish the people for doubting his word. God had earlier showed miracles to them in Egypt and in the wilderness, and had promised them that they would reach the 'land of milk and honey' if they went to war. There is a description of God punishing those who did not believe in him. God commands them to go to war and occupy Canaan (modern-day Israel). The Book of Numbers ends here.

The fifth book is Deuteronomy or Devarim in Hebrew. It means 'words' or 'second teaching'. It describes the last days of Moses. In the first thirty chapters, Moses delivers sermons to the Israelites.* It recounts the forty years of wandering the wilderness and tells people to observe the divine law. It tells them to follow Yahweh (God) so that they can possess the land of Israel. Moses says that if they fall into evil ways, they will lose the land. But by proper repentance, they can regain it. The final chapters contain

---

* Refers to the descendants of Jacob also known as Israel

the Song of Moses and the Blessings of Moses. They emphasize the oneness of God: 'The Lord our God, the Lord is One' (6:4 and 5). The leadership is passed on by Moses to Joshua, and it ends with the death of Moses on Mount Nebo.

The Torah ends with the death of Moses, who led his people to the edge of the Promised Land. It is left to Joshua to take them into Israel.

The Nevi'im or Prophets

This is a largely semi-historical set of texts about the prophets that came after Moses. They had conquered the Holy Land and came into contact with the local people. The locals were settled in agriculture and were more cultured and civilized than the conquering Israelites who came after spending forty years as nomads in the desert. Since the local people followed polytheism and had their own rituals, some of the Israelites were also drawn to that. There was also some intermarrying. The prophets, particularly the Judges, spoke against this and restored the monotheistic faith. There are also prophecies.

Summary of the Principal Contents

We examine the texts first for revelations. There are many examples of this, particularly in the Torah. God never shows His form, but speaks, shows dazzling lights, performs miracles and so on. Some well-known examples are given below.

'And when Abram was ninety years old and nine, the Lord appeared to Abram and said unto him, I am the Almighty God: walk before me and be thou perfect' (Genesis 17:1).

Abraham was earlier known as Abram. The revelation does not describe what Abraham saw, but it says that God appeared and spoke. The exhortation to be perfect is common to all religions. Many centuries later, Christ says, 'Be thou perfect even as your father in heaven is perfect' (Mathew 5:48). The word perfect is not defined. But it most likely refers to living properly, following the moral and ethical codes, not hating anyone, loving everyone and leading a God-centred life. There are several interpretations of this available in later literature. God also appears to Abraham in the plains of Mamre (Genesis 18:1). Elsewhere, God tells Jacob that he shall henceforth be known as Israel.

Exodus has at least 400 references to God speaking to the prophets, principally Moses. It says, 'And the angel of the Lord appeared unto him in a flame of fire out of the midst of a bush; and he looked, and behold, the bush burned with fire, and the bush was not consumed' (Exodus 3:2). This is one of the most famous and most oft-quoted incidents in the life of Moses. At that time, God speaks to

Moses and says, 'I am that I am; and He said, Thus shalt thou say unto the children of Israel, I Am has sent you' (Exodus 3:14). This is also a famous statement from God. Since God is beyond definition, the phrase 'I am that I am' is used. In fact, the Judaic name for God is Yahweh, sometimes written as YHWH, one of the meanings being 'to be'. Along with God revealing Himself to Moses by speaking, the verse also gives a clear concept of God as one that *is*. This is similar to other theistic religions, including Hinduism and Sikhism, Christianity and Islam. In Exodus 6:3, God says, 'And I appeared unto Abraham, unto Isaac, and unto Jacob, by the name of God Almighty, but by my name Yahweh I was not known to them.' The idea that the same God taught earlier people and prophets is also in the Bhagavad Gita (4:1), where Krishna says, 'I taught this eternal science of yoga to the Sun God, Vivasvan, who passed it on to Manu; and Manu, in turn, instructed it to Ikshvaku.' Krishna is not the formless, undefinable God like Yahweh, but the idea that the teaching was ancient is clearly there.

There is a long set of teachings by God including the well-known Ten Commandments. Since they come directly from God, they are considered revelations. By following them we can lead a happier and more meaningful life. There are different sets of specific teachings from God. One set is about immediate action, for instance, God telling Moses to help his people escape Egypt. Another set is God giving the power of various miracles to Moses and Aaron. They use these miracles to show the pharaoh that they can destroy Egypt and also save it. In spite of many miracles, the pharaoh is not convinced as the Lord 'hardened his heart'.

Another set of teachings are about what we would today call rituals. They refer to circumcision, notions of purity and impurity, elaborate instructions about how to conduct worship, how to atone for sins by sacrificing different types of animals and so on. There are other teachings setting down rules governing relations between men and women who are related to each other as husband and wife, son and mother, brother and sister, father and daughter, father-in-law and daughter-in-law, stepson and stepmother and so on. Many of these teachings are culturally specific.

However, there are other universal moral and ethical teachings. The Ten Commandments is one example. All religions agree on most of the basic teachings, including honouring one's parents, not killing, not stealing, not committing adultery, not bearing false witness or coveting the neighbour's wife or property. There is a repeated command to love and worship God. In Deuteronomy 6:5, the well-known teaching is 'Love thy God with all thine heart, soul and might'. This is also universal in all theistic religions. Loving God is taught in all of them. Psychologically speaking, this attitude of love brings peace.

Buddhism and Jainism are not about God, but they also repeatedly teach you to cultivate the feelings of love and compassion for all beings.

Concept of God from the Torah

God is clearly all-powerful, formless and omniscient. He is also a God of justice, who rewards the good and sometimes punishes the wicked. He reveals Himself to selected people or prophets. He speaks to us and to the people of those times through the words of the prophets, who merely convey to us what God told them. God is monotheistic, and polytheism, idol and image worship are forbidden.

God not only delivers justice, He is also full of mercy. Some statements of God are given below.

'. . . showing mercy into thousands of them that love me and keep my commandments' (Exodus 20:6 and Deuteronomy 5:10).
'The Lord is long suffering, and of great mercy, forgiving iniquity and transgression' (Numbers 14:18).

God also says that His teachings should be followed. Those who do not follow the teachings will be punished. The practical teachings are about moral and ethical values as established in the Ten Commandments. In modern terms, this can be interpreted differently. Following moral and ethical actions makes our life easier, while not following them makes life difficult. God also controls 'evil' people. For instance, the phrase 'he hardened the pharaoh's heart' is used repeatedly in Exodus. God is also holy. He says, 'Speak unto all the congregation of the children of Israel, and say unto them, Ye shall be holy, for I the Lord am holy' (Leviticus 19:2). The word holy is left undefined.

So God is not only omnipotent, omniscient and formless, but also delivers justice, is full of mercy and holiness, and teaches us to love.

God also teaches us how we should live. The teachings are for our own good, and help us to be happy and avoid suffering.

Important Teachings

The most famous set of teachings is from the Ten Commandments. They are about practical, everyday life and teach us about the right morals and ethics. They have already been discussed. Some important teachings are about prayer, often in times of difficulty.

Another well-known teaching is from the Torah, Deuteronomy 6.5: 'And thou shalt love the Lord thy God with all thine heart, and with all thy soul, and with all thy might.' This exhortation to love God and to be devoted to him is present in all the theistic religions without exception. If one can really follow this teaching, man becomes purified and one with God. In Leviticus 19:18, the teaching is 'Thou shalt not avenge, nor bear any grudge against the children of thy people, but thou shalt love thy neighbour as thyself: I am the Lord'. Jesus Christ gave the same teaching centuries later when he also says 'Love thy neighbour as thyself'.

A related teaching is from the Ketuvim, Psalm 82:6: 'I (Yahweh) have said, Ye are gods; and all of you are children of the most high.' In Genesis, as mentioned earlier, it is described how God created man and woman in His own image. This is similar to statements of other religions, notably Hinduism, which says that we are all '*amritasya putrah*' or children of God.

If we put these three teachings together, we get a practical basis for religion. All are gods, children of the most high. We must love God with all our heart, soul and might. So we are really loving God, who is our father. Since everyone is a child of God, we love our neighbours as ourselves— they are all our brothers and sisters. This gives a spiritual basis for all moral and ethical teaching. This includes not avenging, bearing grudges, stealing or committing adultery and so on. If we perform such actions, we harm the other children of God. Like other religions, the moral and ethical teachings include not killing, stealing, lying or committing adultery, not hating anyone, not coveting what belongs to others and so on. When we practice these teachings, it purifies the mind and the soul, allows us to live in peace and be happy.

The scriptures also tell us how to pray. More than the words, it is the attitude of mind, the inner feeling that needs to be understood. First, there are a series of teachings about how God's words are very precious. In the Ketuvim Psalm 19:10, it says, 'More to be desired are they (God's teachings) than gold, yea, than much fine gold: sweeter also than honey and the honeycomb.' Some important prayers are Psalm 7:1: 'Lord my God, in thee do I put my trust: save me from them that persecute me, and deliver me.' Praying for strength and for being truthful, Psalm 19:14 says, 'Let the words of my mouth, and the meditation of my heart, be acceptable in thy sight, O Lord, my strength and redeemer.' Psalm 27:1 says, 'The Lord is my light and my salvation; whom shall I fear? The Lord is the strength of my life; of whom shall I be afraid?' If we recall that we must love God with all our heart, soul and might, then we seek nothing else but God. For such a person, there is no fear.

Sometimes, the devotee is celebrating in joy. Psalm 68:4 says, 'Sing to God, sing praises to His name; extol Him who rides on the clouds, by His Name YAH, and rejoice before Him.' These psalms are meant to be sung.

God is also omnipresent. In Psalms, it says:

139:7 Whither shall I go from thy Spirit?
Or whither shall I flee from thy presence?

139:8 If I ascend up into heaven, thou art there:
If I make my bed in Sheol,* behold, thou art there.
139:9 If I take the wings of the morning,
And dwell in the uttermost parts of the sea;
139:10 Even there shall thy hand lead me.

This Psalm also provides a method of thinking about, adoring and praying to God as He is everywhere. These verses in particular are reminiscent of statements of other religions. In the Gospel of Thomas, Jesus Christ says, 'I am the All. Cleave a piece of wood, and I am there. Lift up a stone, and You will find Me there' (77). In the psalms quoted earlier, it says that God is everywhere, but here Jesus says he is everywhere. Jesus identified completely with God, as his statement 'I and my Father are One' show. So the Gnostic Gospel is also saying that God is everywhere. In the Bhagavad Gita, it says 'sarvam āvṛitya tiṣhṭhati' (Chapter 13: 14)—God pervades everything in the universe.

God is also love. In Psalm 136, it says, 'His love endures forever' twenty-six times, once at the end of each line. This is repeated in other verses as well, including in Psalm 25. Similarly, in Christianity, in the Gospel of John, it says, 'God is love, and whoever abides in love

---

* Sheol: a subterranean underworld where the souls of the dead go after the body dies.

abides in God, and God abides in him' (John 1: 46). In Islam, the words *Rahman* and *Raheem* are used. One of the names of Allah is 'Al-Wadud'. All these words show that God is loving, compassionate and always forgiving. In one instance, the Prophet Mohammad says Allah has more love for His servants than a mother has for her child. In Hinduism, it says, '*anirvachaniya prema Swarupma*'— (God) is inexpressible love (Narada Bhakti Sutras, 51).

God is Truth as well. 'Truth is the seal of the Holy One, blessed be He' (Talmud, Shabbat 55a). 'The Lord God is truth' (Jeremiah 10:10), and '. . . speaketh the truth in his heart' (Psalms 15:2).

God is omniscient, omnipresent, love and truth. This is true of all theistic religions. Buddhism and Jainism do not accept God but accept love and truth, and that the enlightened person attains to omniscience. We discuss this in a later chapter.

There are several ethical and moral teachings. For instance, 'This is what the Lord Almighty said: "Administer true justice; show mercy and compassion to one another. Do not oppress the widow or the fatherless, the foreigner or the poor. Do not plot evil against one another"' (Nevi'im, Zechariah, 7: 9-10).

The methods of reaching God are also given. Following the commandments is crucial. Prayer is also added as a powerful means of approaching God. Wisdom that sees everything in its right perspective is also emphasized. In

Ecclesiastes, the word 'vanity' is used at least thirty-three times. For instance:

> Vanity of vanities, says the Preacher,
> vanity of vanities! All is vanity. —Ecclesiastes 1:4

> I have seen all the works that are done under the sun; and, behold, all is vanity and vexation of spirit. —Ecclesiastes 1:14.

In Christianity, Jesus Christ says, 'My Kingdom is not of this world' (John 18:36). Here, the reference is to the Kingdom of God. The Ecclesiastes verses say the same when they say that pursuing the things of the world does not provide any lasting happiness.

Judaism and Some Common Ideas of All Religions

Concepts of creation, heaven, hell and salvation are present in many religions. Genesis tells the story of creation, and this is regarded as holy in Judaism, Christianity and Islam. In the Indian religions, there are myths and legends about creation, particularly in Hinduism in the Puranas. However, the Vedas and the Upanishads, which are considered the holiest texts, do not contain any stories about creation. The Puranas have a secondary status to the Vedas and Upanishads. Buddhism and Jainism do not even accept that there is a creator. Sikhism accepts God as creator but there are no stories of creation in the sacred text.

The word 'salvation' occurs only once in Genesis, twice in Exodus and once in Deuteronomy. But it does not refer to any ultimate destiny of the individual. The word 'heaven' is mentioned several times in Genesis, Exodus and Deuteronomy, but only once in Leviticus, and is not mentioned in Numbers. However, it does not say anywhere that the individual goes to heaven after death or later. The word 'hell' is not mentioned in any of the five texts of the Torah, except once in Deuteronomy, where again it does not refer to any place that the individual goes to after death. So the Torah does not say anything about an individual going to heaven or hell after death.

The Torah does not directly refer to any day of judgement. The Talmud and the Book of Daniel and Isaiah, however, refer to a Day of Judgement when all souls would be resurrected and judged. Some would go to heaven and others to hell. The Abrahamic religions, including Judaism, do not believe in reincarnation. However, some scholars have interpreted some of the sayings of the Torah to mean there is a final day of judgement.

Spiritual Traditions in Judaism

All religions have a spiritual tradition and a conservative aspect. The conservative or traditional aspect of religion is usually dominant in society. The spiritual tradition is confined to a minority. This is true in all religions including the Abrahamic religions, Judaism, Christianity and Islam, as well as in the Indian religions.

In mainstream Judaism, God revealed Himself to the prophets, and from them we get the sacred texts, in particular the Torah. Through these prophets and the sacred books, God taught the people and gave them commandments, telling them what to do and what not to do. By following these teachings, the individual attains God's grace. Direct revelation from God is apparently reserved only for the chosen ones, the prophets, who in turn become teachers of the people. Man's duty is to follow the commandments in the sacred texts.

On the other hand, spirituality is usually understood to be a concern with the human spirit or soul, or with God or some transcendental reality. Mysticism is also part of all religions. Evelyn Underhill says, 'Broadly speaking, I understand it to be the expression of the innate tendency of the human spirit towards complete harmony with the transcendental order.' It is a direct attempt to gain experience of something that is independent of sensory experience or intellectual understanding, and is 'divine'.

Some metaphysical questions naturally arise, either from revelation or from philosophy. What is the final destiny (eschatology) of an individual? Related to this is the question of what happens to the soul (if there is one) after death.

In Judaism, the mainstream religion does not emphasize mysticism, and later conservative scholars have disagreed with some of its tenets. There is no clear agreement on what the ultimate destiny of the individual is. The emphasis seems to be on living the proper life here and now, without delving into the ultimate destiny of the individual, and whether they have a soul or not or what ultimately happens to it.

However, there were spiritual and mystical traditions in Judaism and a few sects following them. The Essene was an ancient Jewish sect, perhaps between 200 BCE and 100 CE. They were a largely monastic community, which lived in small groups separate from the general population. They lived an ascetic life. They observed the Laws of Moses, the sabbath and ritual purity. Greek philosophers like Plato and Pythagoras articulated a theory of reincarnation. In a similar way, the Essene sect accepted the idea of rebirth. They did not agree with the resurrection of the body after death. They believed in an immortal soul, in reincarnation. They accepted the Torah, but their life and search was spiritual. It gave rise to the Kabbalah, which perhaps evolved much later, in medieval times. In the seventeenth century, another sect called the Hasidic Jews came up, which also has a mystical approach to Judaism.

The idea that the individual gets the just results of their actions is in the Hebrew phrase 'mida k'neged mida', meaning measure for measure. However, for mainstream Judaism as well as Christianity and Islam, the results are experienced in this life and not perhaps in some later life, as in Hinduism. There is no rebirth, but there is a concept of resurrection when God resurrects all people and according to one's deeds, you either go to heaven or hell. At a practical level, such a belief encourages everyone to lead a moral and ethical life, and to avoid evil actions. However, some mystic sects of Judaism do not accept this doctrine and in fact, accept the concept of reincarnation and eventual liberation after several lifetimes. The Essenes and the later Kabbalah traditions have the concept of *gilgul*, where souls migrate into new bodies after death. The purpose of several lives is to eventually fulfil all the commandments. After this, the individual attains salvation. The idea of eternal reward or punishment on a day of judgement is absent here. Mainstream rabbis, however, have rejected this idea.

In the spiritual tradition, there are visions. The Torah records several revelations or visions that the prophets, including Moses, received or saw. God repeatedly reveals Himself to Moses. We see this even in the other sacred texts. All these spiritual experiences have been interpreted as accompanied by a change in the prophet who received them, a sense of wonder, and joy or ecstasy. This is considered to be one of the essential aspects of a spiritual experience.* For instance, 'Elisha prayed and said "Hashem,

---

* The interpretation of a vision or revelation as a spiritual experience based on a change of consciousness and of joy or ecstasy may not be accepted by mainstream or conservative traditions in Judaism

I pray to Thee, open his eyes that he may see." And Hashem opened the eyes of the young man, and he saw and behold, the mountain was full of horses and chariots of fire around Elisha' (Kings 2, 6:17).

In Nevi'im or the book of Prophets, there is a section about the Prophet Ezekiel. He says that the spirit took him up, he heard a great rushing, the noise of the wings of living creatures, and 'the hand of the Lord was strong' upon him. He remained in a state of astonishment for seven days (Prophets, Ezekiel, 3:12 to 3:15). In the same book, section 40 contains a long description of a vision of Ezekiel, with the characteristic phrase 'and the hand of the Lord was upon me'. In the Book of Zechariah in Nevi'im, the first chapter is entirely devoted to a depiction of a vision that Zechariah had, where angels and the Lord spoke to him.

Notes

A central tenet of Judaism is monotheism, that there is only one God. This has been repeatedly declared in the sacred texts, and Abraham was the first to receive this teaching from God. The very first commandment in the Ten Commandments is about there being one God. There were several gods before that, and Abraham himself belonged to a polytheistic tradition. He was converted by revelations from God himself.

However, polytheism continued for several centuries after that. Later sacred texts that came several centuries after Genesis continue to condemn polytheism, and there are references to this practice in later texts like Kings and Zechariah. However, polytheism eventually died out. We find the same historical process in Christianity and Islam. Pagan worship was present in pre-Christian Europe as well as in pre-Islamic Arabia. The early monotheists were persecuted in all the three religions. We see this in Judaism, where the Jews were persecuted in Egypt and had to flee. We see persecution of the early Christians. Similarly, the Prophet Mohammad himself had to flee Mecca and go to Medina. Thus, there were conflicts between polytheists and monotheists when the latter first emerged. Ultimately, over the centuries, monotheism replaced polytheism in all the regions where the Abrahamic religions flourished.

Judaism is divided into various sects. Even by the first century CE, there were the Pharisees, Sadducees and Essenes. The Sadducees emphasized the literal and written word of the Torah and the rituals. They believed that some of the rituals could only be conducted in the Jewish Temple—the first one was destroyed in 587 BCE by the Babylonians and the second one was destroyed around 70 CE by the conquering Romans, after the life of Jesus Christ. The Pharisees believed in an oral Torah which was conveyed by Moses but not written down. They also gave more importance to personal conduct than to rituals. The Essenes were a spiritual sect that lived in monasteries and sought mystical experiences uniting them with God. But they also accepted the Torah.

The Mishna was written around the second century CE and consists of the oral Torah, the teachings of Moses that were not put down in writing. Perhaps it was felt that with the continuing persecution of Jews, this tradition would be lost and so it was put down in writing. Later rabbis added their interpretations, and these were also included in the Talmud.

Jewish philosophy was developed throughout the ages. There are references in the Ketuvim, (the Book of Proverbs, Ecclesiastes, Job and the Song of Solomon, also called the wisdom books) and in the philosophy of the Essenes, who emphasized personal experience of God over following the rituals and the texts. Greek was a language that gave respectability to a philosophy in those days, and Philo Judaeus wrote in the first century CE. He was a Jew who was well-versed in Greek philosophy as well. He placed more value on direct experience than on philosophical or theological speculations. Over the centuries, various writings emerged. They were not based only on the ancient Judaic texts but also on Greek philosophy, and in the medieval times on Islam. Judaism shared with Islam the idea of a monotheistic God, rejection of idol worship and a belief in the prophets. Other Judaic philosophers have said some beliefs, like the wrath of God on wrongdoers, were added to preserve the social order.

The important metaphysical questions are also developed into different philosophies—the nature of God, the universe, the ultimate destiny of the human being, whether there is a soul and so on. The sacred scriptures often do not say anything about these questions. They contain history, revelations that God gave to the prophets and commandments or teachings, as well as details about various modes of worship and rituals.

Judaism is unique because it has the concept of the chosen people and the promised land. Those who accepted the sacred texts were the chosen people, and Israel is the promised land. Like all other religions, Judaism today also has various sects. In the twenty-first century, the three major ones are Orthodox, Conservative and Reform Judaism. The Orthodox hold that the Torah and the Judaic Law are of divine origin. They are eternal and unalterable and should be strictly followed. The Conservatives regard the texts as guidelines rather than strict dos and don'ts. Reform Judaism allows interpretation of the sacred texts, and says that the ethical and moral teachings are superior to the rituals. They are also open to other values.

About 0.2 per cent of the world's population follows the religion of Judaism. It is not a proselytizing religion and has no missionaries to convert people. However, it does accept converts. The population is concentrated largely in

Israel and the United States. The ancient texts do not use the word 'Jew'. They are called sons of Israel or Israelites. Many centuries later, they began to be called Jews. It is seen as an ethnic religion, in contrast to universal religions like Buddhism, Christianity and Islam, whose followers are spread around the globe.

2

CHRISTIANITY

A Short Life History of Jesus Christ

Christianity is based on the life and teachings of Jesus Christ. He is regarded as the Son of God, and known as the Messiah, or Christ, derived from the Greek '*Christos*', which means the chosen one or the anointed* one. The principal source of material on the life and teachings of Jesus Christ are the four Gospels of Mathew, Mark, Luke and John. Some of the material is common, while some are unique to each Gospel. The word Gospel originally meant good news or good story. They give the story of Jesus.

Jesus was born in Bethlehem, Israel, to his mother, Mary, in a devout Jewish family. He is said to have been born in the beginning of the Common Era in the year 0 CE. However, the exact year is not known with certainty.

---

* Anointed: made holy in a religious ceremony that involves putting holy water or oil on them (Cambridge Dictionary); implies here that Jesus was anointed by God.

Christians believe that Jesus was born of immaculate conception, i.e., that his mother, Mary, conceived him through the Holy Spirit and was a virgin.* Her then fiancé, Joseph, wanted to leave her, but was instructed by an angel in a dream to marry her. The angel told him that Mary had conceived through the Holy Spirit and that a divine child would be born to her. So Joseph married her.

In the Old Testament, which is the most sacred set of texts for the Jews, there is a saying, 'Therefore the Lord himself shall give you a sign; Behold, a virgin shall conceive and bear a son, and shall call his name Immanuel' (Isaiah 7:14 in the Nevi'im or Prophets). The Gospel of Mathew refers to this statement of Isaiah and says this is the fulfilment of that ancient prophecy. However, mainstream Judaism does not accept this interpretation.

Wise men or *magi* from the East came to know of the birth and followed a star in the sky to find the baby Jesus. They said that the 'King of the Jews' was born. The Roman king Herod summoned the wise men and told them to follow the star and tell him where the baby was so that he could worship it. The magi found the baby and worshipped Jesus. They were told in a vision not to go back to Herod. They understood that Herod was not

---

* There is a similar belief in Buddhism. Buddha was born as Siddhartha Gautama, whose mother Maya conceived him when in a vision a white elephant entered her right side, showing that he was not of ordinary human origin.

really interested in worshipping the baby, but in knowing where it was so he could kill it. Herod ordered all male children born at that time to be killed as he did not want anyone else to be king of the Jews. Joseph was then again instructed in a dream to leave Bethlehem and go to Egypt with his family. The family left at night and went there.* After Herod died, Jospeh was again instructed in a dream to come back to Israel, but to go to Nazareth in Galilee and not return to Jerusalem.

In the Gospel of Luke, there is an incident about Jesus as a child of twelve. His parents, Joseph and Mary, took him from Nazareth to Jerusalem for the Jewish festival of Passover (which celebrates the end of Jewish slavery in Egypt) and stayed for a week. While returning, they discovered that Jesus was missing. They had assumed that he was with the group. They walked back and after a day's search, found him in the Jewish Temple. He was discussing religious issues with the priests there, who were amazed by his knowledge and wisdom. Jesus then went back to Nazareth with his parents.

After that, there is a gap of about eighteen years. They are sometimes called the lost or unknown years. Jesus then appears around the age of thirty. He is baptized by John

---

* Krishna was born in prison and the then king, Kamsa, who was also his maternal uncle, ordered that he should be killed. However, his father Vasudeva escaped with the child at night and saved him.

the Baptist, a holy man who lived in the wilderness, gave solace to people and baptized them with water. He was older than Jesus. John also had a miraculous birth when the angel Gabriel appeared to his father Zechariah and told him that he would have a son, in whom the Holy Spirit would enter from birth (Luke 1:15). John, however, knew that someone greater than him would come, who would baptize people not with water like him, but with the Holy Spirit and fire. Jesus goes to John to get baptized. John recognizes his spiritual greatness and says that in fact, Jesus should baptize him. But Jesus says, let us follow the tradition, and so he is baptized. A voice from heaven is heard saying, 'This is my one dear Son; in him I take great delight' (Gospel of Mathew 3.17). A dove also appeared, and in the Christian tradition, it is the symbol of the Holy Spirit.

Jesus then goes away to the desert to fast and pray for forty days.* At the end, Satan comes to tempt him three times. First, he tells the famished Jesus he can turn the stones into bread. Jesus turns down the temptation by saying, 'Man does not live by bread alone . . .' (Mathew 4:4). Satan then asks him to jump from the mountain, as the angels would save him. Jesus replies, 'You are not to put the Lord thy God to the test' (Mathew 4:7). A third

---

* The Prophet Mohammad also went into the wilderness to fast and to pray.

time Satan tempts him and tells him that he will make him king of the world if only Jesus would worship him, Satan. Then Jesus says, 'Go away, Satan! For it is written: "You are to worship the Lord your God and serve only him"' (Mathew 4:7).*

It is interesting to note that Jesus later miraculously multiples bread and creates wine out of water to feed the crowds gathered around him. But here, he refuses to use this power to turn stone into bread when Satan tempts him. Such powers were used only for the good of the people and never for one's own benefit. In the modern age, many would say that these temptations, whether in the case of Jesus or Buddha or any other sages and prophets, came from their own mind. It was attributed variously to Satan, Mara and some external evil forces.

Jesus returns and starts his ministry. He spoke largely in Aramaic, a semitic language spoken in Galilee and Jerusalem at that time. Various incidents are described in which he first accepts the Apostles, and then accepts other disciples. He continually performs miracles, healing the sick, the blind, the lame and lepers, and bringing those who died back to life. 'The blind see, the lame walk, lepers are cleansed, the deaf hear, the dead are raised, and the poor

---

* In the final moments before getting Nirvana, Buddha is also tempted by Mara, the evil one in many ways. Buddha overcomes all these temptations and attains Nirvana or Buddhahood.

have good news proclaimed to them' (Mathew 11:5). He saves a boat from capsizing by calming and controlling the wind and the turbulent sea. He walks on water, multiplies bread and turns water into wine miraculously and feeds a large number of people. He even blesses those who were considered sinners and redeems them.

In a special incident, three of the Apostles, Peter, James and John, also saw a blinding vision of Jesus, Moses and Elijah. 'And he was transfigured before them. His face shone like the sun, and his clothes became white as light. Then Moses and Elijah also appeared before them, talking with him' (Mathew 17:2–4). This is known as the 'Transfiguration'.

Jesus also gives his spiritual powers to his Apostles. 'Jesus called his twelve disciples and gave them authority over unclean spirits so they could cast them out and heal every kind of disease and sickness' (Mathew 10:1). He singles out Simon Peter and says, 'And I tell you that you are Peter, and on this rock I will build my church, and the gates of Hades will not overpower it. I will give you the keys of the kingdom of heaven' (Mathew 16:18-19). Peter comes from the Greek word *petros* or *petra*, which means rock. Hades refers to a Jewish concept—it is the place where the dead go. He means that even death or hell cannot overpower the church.

As Jesus grows in popularity, large crowds follow him everywhere he goes. He first preaches the famous Sermon on the Mount, which also contain the Beatitudes and the well-known Lord's Prayer.

He gives instructions to the Apostles. 'He summoned the Twelve and began to send them out two by two and gave them authority over unclean spirits. He instructed them to take nothing for the journey but a walking stick— no food, no sack, no money in their belts. They were, however, to wear sandals but not a second tunic' (Mark 6: 7-9).

The traditional priests or rabbis felt jealous of Jesus as his popularity grew. They were always looking for some way to get rid of him. They find one instance where Jesus tells someone that his sins are forgiven and cures him. The priests says that only God can forgive sins, and Jesus was committing blasphemy by claiming to forgive. Jesus also criticized the hypocrisy in religion, further angering the priests. Jesus predicts his own demise to his disciples. In one instance, Jesus enters the Jewish Temple, throws everyone out and denounces the hypocrisy and falsehood practised there. He perhaps found the priests more interested in material things than in God and in correctly guiding the devotees.

Whatever the provocation, they went and complained to Pontius Pilate, who by then was the Roman ruler in charge. Israel was under Roman rule and Pilate was the governor of the region, appointed by Caesar from Rome. Ultimately, Pilate sanctioned the Crucifixion of

Jesus Christ. This was a common form of punishment for criminals in those days. For the rabbis, the crime for which Jesus was punished was blasphemy. For Pilate, the real reason was the growing popularity of Jesus and the fact that the powerful rabbis wanted to crucify Jesus. He decided to accept the rabbis' demands. Judas Iscariot came with a crowd to arrest him. Judas kisses his robe and thus identifies Jesus to the crowd. Jesus is aware of the coming events. When one of his disciples takes up a sword to defend him against the crowd, he tells him to put it down: 'For all who take hold of the sword will die by the sword. Or do you think that I cannot call on my Father, and that he would send me more than twelve legions of angels right now?' (Mathew 26: 52, 53).

Jesus allows events to happen and performs no miracle to save himself. He says that the word of the scripture must be fulfilled, and that God's will must be done. Various interpretations have been given, the most well-known of which is that Jesus Christ gave up his life to atone for the sins of mankind.* But we see yet again that Jesus never uses his powers to save himself. He only uses them for the benefit of others.

---

* This idea of a holy person or prophet or son of God atoning for the sins of others by taking the punishment on himself is present in other religions as well, notably in Hinduism.

Jesus was whipped, and a crown of thorns was placed on his head. He was mocked and abused on the way to Golgotha, the site of crucifixion. The Gospels have different versions of the events of the crucifixion. It is implied that he was stripped and crucified. The Gospel of John says that when Jesus saw his mother and the disciple there whom he loved, he said to his mother, 'Woman, behold, your son' (John 19:26). Then he said to the disciple, 'Behold, your mother.' And from that hour, the disciple took her into his home (John 19:27).

This shows the human side of Jesus who, even on the cross, wanted to provide for his mother. The same Gospel also says that a soldier thrust his spear into the side of Jesus and blood flowed out. In the Gospel of Luke there is the famous statement:

'Father, forgive them; for they do not know what they are doing' (Luke 23:34).

In agony on the cross, he still forgives those who crucified him. This teaching has justly become famous all over the world. Two other criminals were also crucified with him. One of them asks to be saved. 'Jesus, remember me when you come into your kingdom' (Luke 23:42). He replied to him, 'Amen, I say to you, today you will be with me in Paradise' (Luke 23:43). Jesus has spiritual power even at this time to forgive a criminal and in fact, promises salvation to him. His last words before he passed away were 'Father, into your hands I commend my spirit' (Luke 23:46).*

As predicted, Jesus is raised from the dead and appears first to Mary Magdalene and to the other Mary (some interpret this to mean his mother). He tells them to go and call the disciples to a designated mountain back in Galilee. There, the eleven disciples, all except Judas, saw him. His last words in the Gospels asking them to spread the teachings are:

'All authority in heaven and on earth has been given to me. Therefore go and make disciples of all nations, baptizing them in the name of the Father and the Son and the Holy Spirit, teaching them to obey everything I have commanded you. And remember, I am with you always, to the end of the age' (Mathew 28: 19,20). 'Go into the whole world and proclaim the gospel to every creature' (Mark 16:15). 'Thus it is written that the Messiah would suffer and rise from the dead on the third day and that repentance, for the forgiveness of sins, would be preached in his name to all the nations, beginning from Jerusalem (Luke 24:16-17).'

---

* There is a strong Hindu belief that only exceptional people can remember God at the time of death. Jesus was one such. The Hindus also believe that such a person becomes one with God.

The Historical Context

Christianity had its beginnings in Israel. The surrounding population was Jewish. Jesus was born about fourteen centuries after Moses. By then, idol worship had been abandoned by the Jews, replaced by faith in a monotheistic God. However, Israel and the Jews had been conquered several times. For instance, the First Temple was built around 1000 BCE by Solomon, son of David. In the Torah, the word used is 'tabernacle', which was the place where God was worshipped. Such places were also used for performing worship and rituals. Later, around 600 BCE, Josiah decreed that all rituals and worship be conducted at the Temple. The Temple was of great importance to the religion. The Babylonians under Nebuchadnezzar invaded Jerusalem and destroyed the temple around 587 BCE.

Cyrus II of Persia, who later conquered Babylon, allowed the exiled Jews to return to Jerusalem in about 540 BCE. They rebuilt the temple, which came to be known as the Second Temple. Israel was under Persian and later Greek (or Hellenic) rule. The rulers did not interfere with the religion. However, a later Hellenistic ruler, Antiochus IV, looted the Temple in the second century BCE, and desecrated it with a sacrifice to the Greek god Zeus in the Temple. The rabbis later purified the Temple. The Romans then conquered Israel, and in about 57 BC they looted the Temple. However, Herod the Great, the king or representative of the Roman emperor at the time of the birth of Jesus, rebuilt the Temple. It started around 20 BCE and the construction continued for more than four decades. The Temple once again became the centre of Jewish religious life at the time of Jesus. Pilgrims came to the Temple from all over Judea (southern Palestine, as it was then known), especially during Jewish festivals like Passover. In one incident in the Gospel of Luke, the parents of the young Jesus, then twelve years old, came from Nazareth to Jerusalem with other pilgrims for Passover. The second Temple was later destroyed in 70 CE during the Roman-Jewish war. Jesus predicted this in the Gospel of Luke. Jesus was crucified around 33 CE, a few decades before the Second Temple was destroyed. It was never rebuilt.

The Romans were interested in Judea because it was located between Syria and Egypt, two important and prosperous areas under Roman rule. They merely wanted peace in Judea, so that they could protect their real interests, which were in Syria and Egypt. In the Old Testament, it is said that the Israelites had fled to Egypt, where they were enslaved. Although in Judea the Jews were under foreign rule, there is no mention of the Jews being slaves. However, there are records of Roman soldiers exerting their authority over the local people. It is important to note that Jesus was born a Jew.

Thus, Christianity began in a period of relative peace but faced wars and conquests. At the time of Jesus, Judea was under Roman rule. The rabbis (Jewish priests) were powerful. The Roman rulers, including the later Pontius Pilate, who assented to the crucifixion of Jesus, did not want to go against the rabbis. There is disagreement about the economic status of the common people. One view is that, like most agrarian societies of those times, the majority were not well-off and supported a small percentage of the well-to-do through taxes. The latter class included the rabbis. At the time of Jesus, Herod was a Roman Jew, and a 'client' king of the Roman emperor. Like any autocratic power, he preferred to have powerful allies among the people. Thus they gave special rights, land and property to the rabbis. The very fact that he rebuilt the Temple shows that he wanted to keep peace with the rabbis. This is one view, although other scholars disagree with it. The role of the rabbis in getting Jesus crucified is mentioned in the Gospels. There is also mention of tax collectors, one of whom was Mathew, who became an Apostle.

Another view is that it was a more egalitarian society. In any case, it is clear that Jesus himself came from the working class and did not belong to the aristocrats, many of whom were rabbis. However, Jesus was also called rabbi because of his knowledge of the scriptures.

Unlike the Old Testament, which repeatedly prohibits image or idol worship, the New Testament does not mention this. However, it does mention that the rabbis had become corrupt and that they opposed Jesus because of his growing popularity. Jesus was well-versed in the Old Testament and he quotes from it often. He is also tested by the rabbis, who accuse him of going against scripture. But Jesus was able to answer them well, quoting from the very same scriptures. He says, 'Do not think that I have come to abolish law or the prophets; I have not come to abolish them but to fulfil them' (Matthew 5:17).

Jesus was largely preaching to the relatively unlettered, common people. The aristocrats may not have been interested in him in significant numbers. The Apostles were largely drawn from fishermen, although Mathew, a tax collector, was an exception and was educated. Like all prophets, he understood the social situation and the people very well. So he preached to them in a language that they could understand.

Jesus says in the Gospel of Mathew that it is given to a few to understand the secrets of the Kingdom of God, but to others he preached in parables. The few he refers to are not the educated, but those who were fit to follow a completely spiritual path. Many of the Apostles were fishermen. He performed many miracles which convinced the ordinary people, and even the spiritually inclined, that he was something extraordinary. This helped him to spread his teachings. In earlier Biblical times, the prophets of the Old Testament, particularly Moses and his brother Aaron, also performed several miracles to win over the people they were leading. However, in the case of the Prophet Mohammad and Buddha, we find less evidence of miracles. Perhaps the society in those regions at that time did not need miracles to convince them of the truth of the teachings. All this of course presupposes that all founders received divine revelations and that their primary goal was to help the people through their teachings. Miracles were not the main message of their teachings.

Like other major religions, Jesus and the early Christians also faced persecution. Not only Jesus, but nearly all his Apostles were put to death in various ways. The Old Testament says that the Jews were enslaved in Egypt. Even when they went to Israel, led by Joshua after forty years of wandering in the desert, they had to fight the then idol worshipping local population (early Judaism went against existing idol worship and may have faced a backlash). The Prophet Mohammad also fled from Mecca to Medina and lived there for the last ten years of his life because of persecution from the establishment in Mecca, which was then full of idol worshippers. Thus, all the three major Abrahamic religions faced persecution at inception. However, in India, we do not find evidence of the founders and prophets, like Buddha, Mahavira or Guru Nanak, facing personal persecution. However, over time, there were conflicts with pre-existing Hindus.

Jesus's life and teachings no doubt have a universal aspect. However, some of his other teachings can be better understood by keeping the social and historical context in mind. The Jews were under Roman rule, and the population was oppressed. People were not highly educated. Unlike the Old Testament, which describes wars, Christianity arose in a time of relative peace. In Christianity, God shows more love, peace, forgiveness and mercy. In the Biblical (Old Testament) times, God no doubt showed all these aspects, but He also showed his wrath and administered justice.

The Sacred Texts

The Life of Jesus is described in the four Gospels of Mathew, Mark, Luke and John. However, several other books were written about the Life of Jesus (for instance, the Infancy Gospel of Jesus), but are not regarded as canonical, i.e., included in an accepted list of sacred texts.

Mathew was clearly an Apostle of Jesus Christ. He was an eyewitness to many of the events in the Gospel. The famous Sermon on the Mount is found only in this Gospel. Many consider this to be the essence of the teachings of Jesus Christ. Mark and Luke were not Apostles, but lived and moved closely with the Apostles. The Gospel of John is considered by some to be written by the Apostle of Jesus, while other scholars say it may have been written by others who followed John. The first three are called the *synoptic*[*]

---

[*] The dictionary defines synoptic as 'forming a general summary'. Here, it refers to the three Gospels having much in common while the Gospel of John was distinct in many ways.

Gospels, which are largely similar. The Gospel of John contains some other material, like Jesus washing the feet of his disciples at the last supper. Taken together, the Four Gospels give a cohesive picture of the life and teachings of Jesus Christ. All were written in Greek within a century of the passing away of Jesus Christ. Some say that there were Aramaic texts that were later put down in Greek. Mathew and Luke were educated, and perhaps so was Mark. One point of debate among scholars is that John the Apostle was not highly educated and could not have written the Gospel, which has literary Greek. Others argue that some well-educated assistants or disciples of the Apostles may have written them on their behalf after first hearing it from them.

Other than these, the Gospel of Thomas was discovered in 1945 in Egypt. This is not accepted as canonical. It does not have the life of Jesus. Many of the parables are the same as those found in the other Gospels. Some speculate that this was the Apostle Thomas of Jesus, but most others do not accept that. It is also called the Gnostic Gospel. The word gnostic refers to mystical knowledge of God. There is a sense that these are the spiritual teachings of Jesus. This was written in the Coptic language of Egyptian origin, and is also dated from the first century. It contains the teachings of Jesus. It is called Gnostic since it seeks to know God rather than only be devoted to Him. There is another text called the Infancy Gospel of Thomas about the life of Jesus from the age of five to twelve. It was written in the second century or a bit later. It is not accepted as an authentic text. The authors of the two 'gospels' carrying the name of Thomas are also different.

There is a long gap of about eighteen years—between the ages of twelve and thirty—in the life of Jesus. These are sometimes called the lost or unknown years of Jesus. Naturally, several theories have come up about these years. One simply says that Jesus worked as a carpenter, just like his father Joseph. Another theory says that he lived with the Essenes, a monastic group during the lost years. Perhaps it was this group which, by the third century CE, came to be known as the 'Desert Fathers'. Another group of people, including some Western scholars nowadays, claim that Jesus came to India during those years. None of these speculations are accepted by the mainstream churches today. People believe that it is not important as the teachings of Jesus Christ are fully available. We need to focus on those teachings and not on the lost years.

In addition to the Gospels, there are other canonical texts. These were probably formally accepted as canonical in the fourth century CE. The first among these is the second part of the Gospel of Luke, known as 'The Acts'. Then there are the Letters of Paul, James, Peter, John, Jude and the Revelations of John. Formally, the Christian religion also accepts the Old Testament texts as sacred. St Paul played a prominent role in the spread of Christianity, but never met Jesus. He became a follower after some spiritual experiences and revelations. Scholars do not agree on whether all the letters of Peter, James, John and Jude (Thaddeus) were written by the Apostles of Christ or by others who attributed the letters to them. The entire list of canonical books is given in order of precedence, with the most sacred coming first.

List of Canonical Books of the New Testament

The Four Gospels According to Matthew, Mark, Luke and John
Acts of the Apostles, the second part of the Gospel of Luke
Letters of Paul to the Romans, Corinthians (two letters), Galatians, Ephesians, Philippians, Colossians, Thessalonians, and to Timothy (two letters), Titus, and Philemon and the Hebrews

Letter of James
Letters of Peter (two letters)
Letters of John (three letters)
Letter of Jude
Revelation to John

Note: The Christian tradition also accepts the Old Testament texts as sacred. Some of the Letters of Paul are now attributed by later scholars to other followers of Paul who used Paul's name to gain acceptability. The letters are also called Epistles.

The Acts records the events and actions of the Apostles and other early saints. It also includes the acts of Paul, who never met Jesus, but was converted through a revelation. Paul became one of the most important figures in the history of Christianity. Whatever we know about the early history of the Christian church is largely from the Acts. The Letters have moral, ethical and spiritual teachings. They reiterate the divine origin of Jesus. However, they are also about events of the day. The Revelation to John in the first part has moral and spiritual teachings. The final section is full of visions and symbols. Scholars have different interpretations of them. It is not known with certainty who John was, although the traditional belief is that he was an Apostle.

Some of the famous teachings from the Letters are given below. One well known phrase is 'the peace that passes all understanding' (Letter of Paul to the Philippians 4:4–7). This deeper search for inner peace is common to the spiritual traditions of all religions. Buddha, for instance, says that Nirvana is full of peace.

'I urge you therefore brothers by the mercies of God to offer your bodies as a living sacrifice, holy and pleasing to God, your spiritual worship' (Paul's letter to the Romans

12:1). Dedicating everything one has to God is again a common theme in all theistic religions. For instance, in the Bhagavad Gita Chapter 4, verse 28, it says, 'Some offer their wealth as sacrifice (*yajna*), while others offer *tapa* or austerities as yajna. Some offer yogic practices as yajna, some study the scriptures and offer knowledge as sacrifice, while observing strict vows.'

'Do you not know that your body is a temple of the Holy Spirit . . . ?' (Letter 1 Corinthians 6:19). Again, this idea that the Holy Spirit resides in human beings is present is other religions too. In the Upanishads, it says repeatedly that the Atman resides in the heart.

'There is neither Jew nor Gentile, neither slave nor free, nor is there male and female, for you are all one in Christ Jesus' (Paul's Letter to the Galatians 3:28). This again reiterates a central teaching of all religions that all people are united in God. Differences of race, language and gender are of no relevance.

'Humble yourselves under God that He may lift you up in due time. Cast all your anxieties on him because He cares for you' (Peter's Letter 1, 5: 6–7). In the Bhakti or devotional traditions of Hinduism, one must give up the ego and surrender it to God. Even an agnostic religion like Buddhism exhorts people to be egoless—in fact, it defines ego-lessness as Nirvana.

'For prophecy never had its origin in the human will, but prophets, though human, spoke from God as they were carried along by the Holy Spirit' (Peter's Letter 2, 1: 21). Here St Peter is saying what all regions claim—that prophets are messengers of God.

Early Christian History

The spread of Christianity started after Jesus. His last words in the Gospel of Mathew were to make disciples of all the nations. In the Gospel of Mark, there are two references: 'But the gospel must first be preached to all nations' (Mark 13: 10), and 'Go into the whole world and proclaim the gospel to every creature' (Mark 16: 15). The Apostles carried out this teaching. Jesus had given them the power to heal and to perform miracles.

The Acts is about events and the acts of the Apostles after the death of Jesus. In the place of Judas, who had betrayed Jesus, another Apostle, Mathias, was selected. The orthodox Jews rejected the Christians, and St Stephen was stoned to death. The Apostles moved away from Jerusalem* and moved to other places to preach to the Gentiles (the non-Jewish people) and to the Samaritans with whom the Jews of that time had serious differences. The Acts records that Peter went to Samaria, Lydda, the

---

* The early Muslims, including the Prophet Mohammad and his followers, were also persecuted in Mecca and went away to Medina. Mohammad lived the last twenty years of his life there, coming back to Mecca once in his last year.

Mediterranean coastal area of Joppa and converted people to the Christian faith. All this was within a radius of less than 200 km from Jerusalem. He also had the power to heal the sick. He converted Cornelius, a 'centurion', who was a Roman officer in charge of a hundred men. This was said to be the first major conversion among the Gentiles. It played a crucial role in spreading Christianity.

Saul, who became Paul after conversion, was a Jew who also persecuted the early Christians. He never met Jesus, but was converted by visions and became a dynamic preacher. Most of the Letters in the canonical texts are from Paul. The Acts also recounts the travels of Paul and how he established various churches. The Apostles of Christ at that time remained in Judea and it was agreed that they would preach to the Jews, and Paul would preach to the Gentiles. His final trip was to Rome, where he continued to preach. He was imprisoned there and according to one tradition, was put to death by the Roman emperor Nero. Much of the early history of the Christian church comes from the book of Acts. The Letters of Paul reiterate the teachings of Jesus. Paul became a central figure in the history of Christianity for the work he did in spreading the teachings of Jesus.

All the Apostles and Paul travelled to preach. James was said to have been killed by Herod (who was the son of Herod the Great, who was the ruler at the time of the birth of Jesus). There is no clear account of what happened to the other Apostles. However, it is widely believed that nearly all of them were eventually killed. John the Baptist, though notionally not a Christian, nevertheless accepted Jesus as a great Messiah. He was also beheaded by Herod the Great in the lifetime of Jesus. It shows that the early Christians were persecuted.

Christianity started spreading rapidly in the fourth century after the Roman emperor Constantine converted to Christianity in 312 CE. His successor established Christianity as the official religion of the state. Prior to this, the Romans had several gods, including Jupiter, Juno and Minerva. There was a prevalent cult of Apollo, apparently borrowed from Greece. It is interesting to note that Buddhism also spread after the conversion of the emperor Ashoka a few centuries after the passing away of the Buddha. In the case of Islam, the Caliph of Baghdad had already converted during the life of the Prophet. Conversion of the ruler helped to spread the religion as the religious and spiritual preachers were no longer persecuted. Constantine issued the Edict of Milan, forbidding the persecution of Christians.

Sects within Christianity

As the religion spread, there were different groups. Even at the time of the Apostles, there was a difference of opinion about whether the Gentiles who converted to Christianity had to follow the Laws of Moses and the Jewish rituals. One group led by James and perhaps endorsed by Peter favoured such a conversion. Paul, however, differed (although he himself had been a devout Jew before his conversion) and said that Gentiles need not follow the Mosaic Law.

The earliest attempts at ecumenism (i.e., a unification of the Church) were in the fourth century CE. Seven ecumenical councils were held between the fourth and seventh centuries CE. They were all held in Istanbul, in what is now called Turkey. They went into theological issues and declared that Christ was the 'only begotten Son of God'. The councils also went into questions of whether Christ was purely divine or was both human and divine. Several decrees were made at each of the councils.

In the eleventh century there was a major schism which created the Roman Catholic Church and the Eastern Orthodox Church. The latter refer to themselves as the Orthodox Catholic Church. The major differences are theological. The Latin term *filioque*, meaning 'and from the Son', is added to the creed that the Holy Spirit comes from God. The Eastern Church believes that the Holy Spirit comes only from God, while the Roman Catholic Church believes that the Holy Spirit comes from God the Father, and through Jesus Christ the Son. The Eastern Church does not believe in the supremacy of the Pope, while the Roman or Western Church does. Recent attempts in the twentieth and twenty-first centuries have tried to play down these doctrinal differences between the churches.

Another major schism was the reformation. Various attempts at reforming the Church had been made down the centuries. However, the major figure is Martin Luther who, in 1517, was believed to have nailed his 'Ninety-five Theses' to the main door of his church. Several copies of the book were sold in Germany, and it apparently became popular with the people. It talked of various issues within the church that required reform. One was the sale of 'indulgences'. A person could go to a priest, confess his or her sins and gain remission for the sins by paying a fine. This was known as an indulgence. Martin Luther questioned this and other practices. He was tried for this in 1521 and was excommunicated. However, his life was spared.

Martin Luther began lecturing. He said that faith in God and Jesus Christ was enough. Jesus Christ was the saviour and had already paid for our sins though his life and crucifixion. He criticized the church for asking people to do good works and for penances.

Martin Luther got married to a nun, putting the seal of approval on clerical marriage. Several other priests also married former nuns. Luther said that celibacy was against the teachings of the Bible, largely using the Old Testament to argue his point of view. This was another major departure from the Church—both the Eastern and the Western

Churches insisted on celibacy for ordained bishops. They point to a saying of Jesus: '. . . some who became eunuchs for the sake of the kingdom of heaven. The one who is able to accept this should accept it' (Mathew 19:11). There is no real dispute since Jesus says 'some become eunuchs', not all.

Within the Catholic Church headquartered in the Vatican, and called the Roman Catholic Church, there are twenty-three other Eastern Churches based in various countries of Africa, Asia, and Europe. They differ in the rituals they practice, but accept the 'papal' authority of the Pope in the Vatican. This supremacy is based on the doctrine that there is a succession of Popes from St Peter the Apostle to the Pope in the Vatican.

The Eastern Orthodox Church or the Orthodox Catholic Church has its headquarters in Istanbul, formerly Constantinople, in present-day Turkey. Their churches are also spread over various countries in South-east and Eastern Europe, North Asia, Egypt, the Near East, Cyprus and even Northern America. They do not have the concept of 'papal' supremacy, and simply follow their doctrines. However, the bishop in Istanbul is given some precedence. At the same time, some countries have declared independence, like the Russian Church.

The Protestants also divided into various churches or sects. These include Anglican, Reformed, Lutheran, Methodist, Pentecostal and Baptist. Some other well-known sects are the Quakers and Presbyterians. Several Protestant churches were established as they do not look for acceptance by any of the Catholic Churches. In a sense, this is similar to Hinduism, where there are married priests in temples, but celibate monks in monasteries.

Language also varied. Greek was used earlier, and later Latin. The population or lay devotees in the congregation did not understand these languages. The term 'Greek Orthodox Church' is often used to refer to the use of the Greek language in the Eastern Orthodox Church. In the Roman Catholic Church, Latin was used. Later worship started being conducted in local languages. Jesus neither preached in Greek nor in Latin. He preached in Aramaic, the spoken language at that time. However, the New Testament was in what is called Koine Greek, an offshoot of Greek. The Old Testament was originally in Hebrew.

However, churches and sects agree that Jesus Christ was a Messiah, the Son of God, and that praying to him and accepting him has great religious and spiritual merit.

Theology

Christian theology is based on the life and teachings of Jesus Christ, and on the Old Testament. Later, there were Greek and even Islamic influences on the development of theology. Theology is defined as 'the study of the nature of God and religious belief'. In the case of Indian religions like

Hinduism, Buddhism and Jainism, the word philosophy is used instead of theology. Theology was perhaps first articulated in the earliest ecumenical councils between the fourth and sixth centuries, and by various saints and scholars. Even today, there are many schools of divinity in various universities that study theology. Many Christian sects make their priests, monks or nuns go through courses in theology. It should be noted that Jesus was not a theologian. He spoke the truth but did not create any theology or philosophy. That was left to the later followers and scholars.

The concept of the Holy Trinity, a major theological concept, can be traced to Jesus himself. He speaks of God as Father and refers to himself as the Son of Man several times. The Holy Spirit entered Mary and she became pregnant. John the Baptist refers to Jesus and says, 'He will baptize you with the Holy Spirit and fire' (Mathew 3:11). The very last teaching he gives after resurrection to the Apostles is 'Therefore go and make disciples of all nations, baptizing them in the name of the Father and the Son and the Holy Spirit' (Mathew 28:19).

Many of the early ecumenical councils went into the question of what the Father, Son and Holy Spirit mean. While Judaism and Islam believe in monotheism, Christian theology has used the concept of the Holy Trinity. God, though the same as the Jewish Yahweh, cannot be comprehended and is a mystery. This can be revealed through special revelation. God is the Trinity—God as Father, as Son and as the Holy Spirit. The infinite God is beyond definition. The Holy Spirit is a divine force or breath, *ruah*,* that resides in everyone—especially those who accept Jesus Christ: 'The Kingdom of God is within you' (Luke 17:21). However, there are differing interpretations and understandings of the Holy Spirit, sometimes also called the Holy Ghost or Paraclete. This also ties in with the sayings of the Gospels like 'No one knows the Son except the Father, and no one knows the Father except the Son and anyone to whom the Son decides to reveal him' (Mathew 11:27). Jesus Christ as a special revelation tells us who God (the Father) is. Critics of Christianity say that this is like polytheism. In Hinduism also, the special revelations or messengers of God (called avatars) can help us to know what God is. Various doctrines and writings have explained the concept of the Holy Trinity.

There was Hellenic and, in later times, Islamic influence on the development of Christian theology. One well-known example is Thomas Aquinas, a monk, who developed a philosophy and theology. He used Greek philosophy, reason and the New Testament to develop his ideas. He was also said to be a mystic with direct spiritual experiences and a great devotee of Jesus Christ. He along

---

* 'Ruah' or 'ruach' is a Hebrew term that means breath or spirit of God.

with four others, Ambrose, Augustine of Hippo, Jerome and Gregory were the early 'Doctors of the Church', a formal recognition of their doctrines. This was done after they were conferred sainthoods.

Even within devout and serious followers of religion, there are people of different temperaments, different personal approaches to God. Even if they all revere the founder, in this case Jesus, they understand his teaching in different ways. This is the basis of theological differences and of different churches. In this book, we give primary importance to the life and teachings of Jesus Christ. Since the sayings are simple and direct, each person can understand them in their own way.

Spiritual and Mystical Traditions

There was a continuous stream of spiritual seekers, even from Biblical times. The terms mystic and gnostic also indicate a quest for direct spiritual experience. In the western way of understanding, the mystic seeks it through devotion, while the gnostic does so through reason and knowledge. The commandments, parables, ethical and moral teachings, as well as rituals, were accepted by the majority, but they may not lead to what the mystic or gnostic seeks. The majority of followers gave less importance to the spiritual teachings.

However, there was always a small minority who were interested in personal spiritual experiences, perhaps even transformative experiences. There was a pre-existing Judaic tradition among the Essenes who lived away from society in monasteries. It is clearly mentioned that John the Baptist lived in the wilderness, and that Jesus also went away into the wilderness for forty days after he was baptized. We can trace this spiritual tradition to some of the sayings of Jesus. If we first see his sayings about God and man, some of them are:

Luke17: 21 'Behold, the kingdom of God is within you.'
Matthew 5:8, 'Blessed are the pure in heart, for they will see God.'

For the serious spiritual seeker, this means that any sincere aspirant can experience God. Then Jesus talks of giving up everything for the sake of God. In the Sermon on the Mount in the Gospel of Mathew, Jesus tells us not to hanker after material things, to depend on God and seek first the Kingdom of God. He also promises what will happen if you do that: 'Ask and it will be given to you; seek and you will find; knock and the door will be opened for you' (Mathew 7:7). He is telling us that an earnest seeker can know the Kingdom of God.

Jesus repeatedly talks of his relationship with God, and with the people: 'Do you not believe that I am in the Father and the Father is in me? The words that I speak to you I do not speak on my own. The Father who dwells in me is doing his works. Believe me that I am in the Father and the Father is in me, or else, believe because of the works themselves' (John 14:10-11), ' I am in my Father and you are in me and I in you' (John 14:20). Mystics seek union with the Spirit or God and Jesus refers to this here.

By the third century CE, there is record of what are now called the Desert Fathers, a spiritual tradition among the early Christians. This was a Christian monastic sect that went into the deserts around Egypt and lived a life of prayer and contemplation. They spread to Egypt, Syria and some regions along the Nile. Some lived in isolation, and others in monastic communities. One of the books they left behind was a compilation of various sayings and writings called *Apophthegmata Patrum* or Sayings of the Desert Fathers. One of the early persons who went into the desert was influenced by Christ saying that we must sell all we have, give to the poor and 'you shall have treasures in heaven'. There was a separate tradition of Desert Mothers as well.

The Eastern Orthodox Church has a set of books called *Philokalia* (Greek: love of the beautiful). It is a collection of books compiled between the fourth and the fifteenth century by various mystics. They talk of the contemplative life. There are also teachings about 'ceaseless prayer' and the Jesus prayer 'Lord Jesus Christ have mercy on me' (English translation). It is said that after the Bible, no other book has had a greater influence on the Orthodox Church than the *Philokalia*. The mystical tradition Hesychasm is related to this (Greek: *hesychia* or stillness). It seeks to still the mind through ceaseless prayer. Some of the Desert Fathers include Paul of Thebes, Antony the Great, St Amun and Abba Or.

Other spiritual persons from the Eastern Orthodox Church include Gregory Palamas, Daniil Sihastrul, Dorotheus, Gerasimus, Joseph the Hesychast and Seraphim of Sarov. Seraphim brought the monastic teachings to lay people recently in the late eighteenth and early nineteenth centuries. He taught that the purpose of Christian life was to receive the Holy Spirit. He also said that if we acquire a peaceful spirit, thousands around us would benefit.*

Several people have been conferred sainthood by the Roman Catholic Church. The lives and writings of some of them reveal that they were mystics. Some of them include St Francis of Assisi, Brother or Deacon Lawrence, Thomas of Kempis who wrote the *Imitation of Christ*, St John of the Cross, St Ignatius Loyola (who founded the Society of Jesus, also knows as the Jesuits), St Catherine of Sienna and St Neot. All of them wrote books that are studied by serious seekers even today.

---

* In Hinduism, the Holy Spirit is understood as the indwelling Atman or divinity. Shanti or peace is obtained for one who knows It.

A few important books in this tradition include *The Way of the Pilgrim* or the *Pilgrim's Tale*. Scholars later inferred that it was written by two Russian monks, Michael Kozlov and Arsenius Troyepolsky, who spent a large part of their life wandering around without a home. Kozlov also wrote about 'ceaseless prayer'. It mentions the Jesus prayer. This is similar to traditions in other religions of repeating a sacred formula or mantra.

Important Teachings of Jesus

The rabbis ask Jesus what the most important teaching is. He says, 'Love the Lord your God with all your heart, with all your soul and with all your mind. This is the first and greatest commandment. The second is like it: "Love your neighbour as yourself." All the law and the prophets depend on these two commandments' (Mathew 22: 37–40).

One way is to look at his teachings as a progression through various stages. First, he proclaims his divinity. He also says on a few occasions that man's inner nature is divine, that (s)he has the 'Holy Spirit'. Then he tells us the way to reach God. Scattered throughout are his teachings in parables, which are meant for those who do not want to follow the purely spiritual teachings—as he says, few can understand the secrets of the Kingdom of God. For the rest, he tells parables, with moral and ethical teachings.

Divinity of Jesus

Here we quote what Jesus himself said in the Gospels rather than what others said about him.

First, he says he does as his father has told him to do. This was common to other prophets before and after Jesus. For instance, he says '. . . I love the Father and that I do just as the Father has commanded me' (John 14: 31). He also says, 'And I know that his commandment is eternal life. So, what I say, I say as the Father told me' (John 12:50). 'The words that I speak to you I do not speak on my own. The Father who dwells in me is doing his works' (John 14: 10). 'I did not speak on my own, but the Father who sent me commanded me what to say and speak' (Mark 12: 49)

From doing what God the Father has told him to do, he goes onto proclaim his identity with God. In the Gospel of John, he says, 'I and my Father are one' (John 10:30). Earlier he says, 'I am the light of the world. Whoever follows me will not walk in darkness but will have the light of life' (John 8: 12). 'I am the way and the truth and the life. No one comes to the Father except through me' (John 14: 6). 'But that you may know that the Son of Man has authority to forgive sins on earth' (Mark 2: 10). According to the rabbis, this was blasphemy as only God had the power to forgive sins.

The Church has emphasized Jesus, the Son of Man (as he often calls himself), as one who is part of the Holy

Trinity of God. This is where the earlier Judaism and later Islam differ from Christianity. They accept Jesus as a prophet, but not as Son of God.

He then goes on to teach about the inherent divinity in man—or rather, the possibility of the Holy Spirit entering man. He says, 'Is it not written in your law, "I said, 'You are gods'?"' (John 10: 34). Here Jesus refers to the Old Testament saying, 'I said, "You are "gods"; you are all sons of the Most High' (Psalms 82:6). Another well-known verse is 'The Kingdom of God is within you' (Luke 17:21).

The Way

For the serious spiritual seeker, the question remains: how do we know this divinity? First, he gives the principles 'Thou shalt know the truth, and the truth will set you free.' Following the truth is then important. He gives some hints. 'My Kingdom is not of this world' (John 18: 36). In various ways he says, do not look for peace in hankering after things of the world. His well-known saying 'It is easier for a camel to pass through the eye of a needle than a rich man to enter the gates of heaven' seems a bit harsh but it was said to a rich young man who persisted in knowing the Kingdom of God. When Jesus tells him of the Biblical commandments, the young man says he has followed them but found no peace. Jesus tells him to sell all he has, give to the poor, that he will have riches in heaven and to follow him. The young man hangs his head and goes away as he could not do that. That is when Jesus says this. He also says, 'You cannot serve God and money (mammon)' (Mathew 6:21). He also tells us not to judge others, to forgive, not to hate anyone. When Peter asks him whether he should forgive someone who wrongs him seven times, Jesus answers, 'I say to you, not seven times but seventy-seven times' (Mathew 18:22). 'You have heard that it was said, "Love your neighbour" and "hate your enemy". 5:44 But I say to you, love your enemy and pray for those who persecute you' (Mathew 5:43). In a sense, these are things that we should not do or what we should give up or not hanker after. An agitated mind, full of desire, anger or hatred, is not able to focus on God. These teachings help us to be free of negative thoughts and keep the mind calm. They also elevate the mind.

Jesus talks repeatedly of love. During the Last Supper he says, 'I give you a new commandment: love one another. As I have loved you, so you also should love one another' (John 13: 34). He also says that we must love God and our neighbour—in fact, he says these are the two greatest commandments. He gives another teaching: 'Blessed are the pure in heart, for they will see God' (Matthew 5:8). Later saints and theologians have interpreted this in various ways to understand what purity of heart means. He says, 'If you love Me, follow my commandments' (John 14:15). It is more than likely that he gave private instructions to the

Apostles, which are not recorded in the Gospels. Fired by these teachings, several people followed them and after a long period of struggle, became saints and mystics.

For others who did not seek spiritual experience, he teaches morals, ethics, forgiveness, love and avoiding hate. His various parables illustrate that.

Notes

For many centuries, Christianity has had the largest number of followers in the world. Jesus explicitly told the Apostles to spread the teaching to all nations. This was true for Islam and earlier for Buddhism as well. Before Christianity, Buddhism was the largest religion in the world. Today, Islam is the fastest growing religion. The Four Gospels are short compared to the sacred texts of other religions like Hinduism and Buddhism, where there are several lengthy books. Judaism, Hinduism, Jainism and Sikhism do not have a tradition of converting people to their faith. However, they also accept those who follow their teachings. Christianity is largely based on devotion to God in Jesus Christ. The Christian view is that anyone can reach God by accepting Jesus as the Son of God and following his teachings.

3

ISLAM

A Short Life History of the Prophet Mohammad

Islam was founded by the Prophet Mohammad, who was born in 570 CE in Mecca in what is now Saudi Arabia. He received the word of God or Allah through the angel Gabriel over a period of several years, starting from around 610 CE to 632 CE, when he passed away. These revelations, called *wahy* in Arabic, were recorded and compiled into the Quran. This is the holiest scripture in Islam.

The main sources of the life of the Prophet are from biographies written by Ibn Ishaq, who lived from around 704 CE to 768 CE; ibn Hisham, who died around 834 CE, and Ibn Tabari (839 CE to 923 CE). The earliest work of Ibn Ishaq is not available, but the later biographies were based on it. Ibn Hashim left out events that could not be verified and also those that had nothing to do with the life of the Prophet. Ibn Tabari's biography is part of a monumental work on history, starting from the prophets of the old Testament and ending with his own times. It has special sections on the life of the Prophet Mohammad. Since Ibn Ishaq was born more than seventy years after the passing away of Prophet Mohammad, he had to rely on the accounts of people who themselves might have heard about Mohammad from a previous generation. The Quran itself has very little information on the life of the Prophet. Another sacred text called the Hadith (Arabic for report of events) has sayings and deeds of the Prophet, as well as other material that had his tacit approval. This was an oral tradition that was later put down in writing. The Sunnah is part of the Hadith and contains traditions and practices of the Prophet.

Mohammad was born to Amina bint Wahb and Abdulla ibn Al-Muttalib. The family belonged to the Hashim clan of the Quraysh tribe. It is believed that the child was a descendant of Ishmael, one of the sons of the Prophet Abraham. Mohammad's father was the son of Abdul Muttalib, a leader of the Quraysh tribe. He died before his son was born. His grandfather named him Mohammad, which means 'praiseworthy'. The Quran says, 'Jesus, son of Mary said: "Oh Israelites, I am Allah's messenger to you, I verify the Torah before me, and I give you the glad tidings of a messenger who shall come after me, his name is Ahmed"' (Quran 61:6). Ahmed also means the one who is praised, and Islamic scholars say that Ahmed refers to the Prophet Mohammad. The Quran therefore says that

Jesus predicted the birth of the Prophet Mohammad. It is interesting to note that the Quran accepts Jesus as a prophet, as well as the ancient Torah, the sacred book of Judaism.

As per the custom of those days, he spent two years with his foster mother, Halima, in the desert. They belonged to the Bedouin tribe. It was a practice among the well-to-do families of Mecca to send their babies to the desert with a wet nurse because the air was pure and would make the child healthy. Another reason was that the child would pick up pure Arabic as the language in Mecca was mixed. For the aristocratic families in Mecca, it was necessary to learn pure Arabic. When the child was returned to the family, the foster parents would be suitably rewarded. Halima, his foster mother, and her family were poor. She decided to adopt the fatherless Mohammad even though it was felt that they would not get much of a reward from the family of a fatherless child. However, Halima's family became prosperous after they adopted the child. Their camels and goats yielded milk in large quantities, and the goats also grew big and strong. This is attributed to blessings from the future prophet.

During this time, there was a miraculous incident when an angel came and cut open Mohammad's heart and removed a clot from it. It is believed that some evil from Satan had been taken away and he became purer. At around the age of four, Mohammad returned to live with his mother Amina. However, within two years, his mother died. He was then brought up by his grandfather, who also died two years later, when Mohammad was eight years old. Before passing away, his grandfather appointed one of his sons, Abu Talib, as his successor and leader of the Quraysh, and told him to look after Mohammad. By the time Mohammad was eight, he had been brought up by four different guardians.

His uncle was a merchant and took the young Mohammad with him on some of his trading trips even as far away as Syria, which is about 2,000 km way from Mecca. In those days, they travelled by camel. The route also passes through Jerusalem. The young boy therefore saw a lot of the outside world, met people of different countries and also learnt the trade. He earned a reputation for honesty and was known as 'al-Amin' or trustworthy, and 'as-Sadiq' or truthful. Traders sometimes kept their gold and wealth with him, knowing that they would get it all back. He was good-looking, of medium height, intelligent and well-behaved. He was also recognized by a Christian monk, Bahira, as a future prophet during these travels. He apparently saw some signs, including the bending of a tree to give shade to Mohammad and a cloud following him in the hot desert.

Since he was honest and intelligent, he was hired by Khadija, a wealthy widow, to trade on her behalf. She was so impressed by him that she wanted to marry him, and he agreed. He was about twenty-five years old and Khadija was about forty years old when they were married in 595 CE. However, some scholars have given different ages. The mainstream Sunni sect of Muslims hold that Mohammad had four daughters and two sons through Khadija. According to the Shia tradition, however, he had only one daughter. The other three were Khadija's sister's children and were adopted when she died. The Sunnis hold that much later, he had a son through Maria al-Qibtiyya. All his sons died in infancy. He also adopted another son. Mohammad was married to Khadija for about twenty-five years and during this time, he never took any other wife, though polygamy was common at that time.

Mohammad started going into seclusion to pray and fast. He went to the cave Hira, Arabic for diamond, on Jabal al Noor, the hill of light. After some time, he started getting revelations through the angel Gabriel (Arabic: Jibrail). The cave is at a height of over 600 metres and about 4 hours way from the Kaaba in Mecca. The night he received the first revelation in the year 610 CE is called the 'night of power'. He was about forty years old then. The angel Gabriel asked him to recite the first three verses of the Quran. He was asked to read, but replied three times that he could not read. But he got the revelation orally anyway:

'In the name of Allah, the Gracious, the Merciful. Convey thou in the name of thy Lord who created man from a clot of blood. And convey thy Lord is Most Generous, who taught man by the pen' (Quran 96:1–5, Surah Al-Alaq).

On his way down, he heard Gabriel say, 'You are a Messenger of Allah, and I am Gabriel.' He came back home trembling. Perhaps the revelation was very powerful. His wife Khadija comforted him and said his experience was that of a prophet. She went to her cousin, who was either a Christian or well-versed in the ancient scriptures. When he heard about Mohammad's experiences, he also said that Mohammad was a prophet. Mohammad's cousin Ali was only eleven, and he also accepted Mohammad. Mohammad's adopted son Zaid, whom he had freed from slavery, also accepted Mohammad. Abu Bakr, a wealthy and honest merchant, also did so. They were the first to accept that Mohmmad had received divine revelations. However, his uncle Abu Talib could not give up the religion of his ancestors, who worshipped idols, but allowed his son Ali to accept Allah.

After that, the revelations stopped for some time, and Mohammad was unhappy. He felt that Allah had left him. However, the angel Gabriel appeared again and reassured him that Allah was pleased with him. He was told to start preaching. In the initial years, he preached only to a close circle of friends. He would continue to get revelations from time to time. He would recite them to his close circle and they would either memorize it or write it down. It is said that when the revelations came, he would break into a sweat and sometimes tremble or shiver.

The early followers were few in number, and they used to go with Mohammad to pray outside Mecca. However, the angel Gabriel then came and told Mohammad to preach openly to the public. He started doing so, but was initially met with ridicule. However, as more people slowly started following him, the merchants became hostile. At that time, the Kaaba had 360 idols, perhaps one for each day of the lunar calendar. When Mohammad started preaching about Allah and asked people to stop idol worship, perhaps the powerful families in Mecca felt slighted. Some of their workers converted to Islam, and they felt threatened. So they started persecuting the early Muslims.

However, his uncle Abu Talib was a leader of the Quraysh and protected him. So they started persecuting the weak and poor followers of Islam. A few of them left and went to Abyssinia. This is called the first *hijra* or migration. The King of Abyssinia gave them protection.

The leaders decided to kill Mohammad but Abu Talib's sons protected him. The leaders then decided to enforce an economic and social boycott of the Muslims. This weakened the Muslims. However, at a spiritual level, this actually strengthened Islam as Mohammad got more revelations during this period. In the year 619 CE, Khadija passed away. This is called the year of mourning as she was the first person who accepted Islam and was beloved of the Prophet. Soon after that, Abu Talib also died. This meant that the protection he gave to the Prophet was gone. The persecution increased. Mohammad decided that he would leave Mecca. He first went walking to Taif, but the people there derided him. However, he got a revelation there that further strengthened his faith in Allah.

On his return to Mecca, he had a very significant experience. He was taken by a winged horse to Jerusalem. This is called the Isra or night journey from Mecca to Jerusalem. There he met Jesus, Moses and Abraham, the earlier prophets, and also prayed there. From there, he ascended to heaven on the horse. This is called Miraj or the Ascent from Jerusalem to Heaven. Along the way, he saw Jesus again and many of the ancient prophets. He was in the presence of the light of Allah. Here, he received a significant revelation which in part says, 'We make no distinction between any of His messengers' (Quran 2: 285, Surah al-Baqarah). There, Allah asks Mohammad to teach the people to pray five times a day.

In 622 CE, Mohammad went with Abu Bakr to Yathrib, now called Medina, where his followers had already migrated. This year is known as the year of hijra, and the Islamic calendar begins at this time. The *azan* or call to prayer, starting with the words 'Allah O Akbar' (God is great), was started here. This called all Muslims to pray.

The tradition of facing Jerusalem while praying was also changed, and Muslims now faced Mecca while praying. Medina had some Jews who, like the Muslims, did not believe in idol worship.

The Muslims in Yathrib had a very difficult time as they had left their belongings back home in Mecca and did not have sufficient means of earning a living. They took to raiding the caravans from Mecca as they travelled for trade. This may have led to further tensions with the Quraysh in Mecca.

It led to the Battle of Badr, fought in 624 CE, and is mentioned in the Quran also. Mohammad prayed for victory before the battle. Though vastly outnumbered, the Muslims won. Muslims believe that divine intervention, and the prayers and genius of the Prophet, helped them defeat the Meccans, even though they were completely outnumbered. It consolidated Mohammad's reputation and several tribes accepted him and Islam after that. It is said that Mohammad planned the battle but did not personally participate in it and spent his time in prayer.

The Meccans attacked the Muslims and defeated them in the Battle of Uhud in 625 CE. One section of soldiers disobeyed the Prophet and the Muslims paid the price. The third battle, called the Battle of the Trench, was fought when the Meccans came with a much larger force of about 10,000 men. This was another victory for the Muslims, where again it is believed that divine intervention helped them. The period between 624 CE and 628 CE was a period of battles.

Later, Mohammad had a dream where he was asked to make a pilgrimage to Mecca. He went with his followers, dressed in white and without arms. On the outskirts of Mecca, they met some official messengers from Mecca and signed a peace treaty. They then went to Mecca and prayed at the Kaaba. This is known as the lesser pilgrimage or Umra. The treaty also allowed them to return again for pilgrimages. Meccans who wanted to join Islam with the permission of their family were allowed to do so. Similarly, those Muslims who wished to return to Mecca and leave Islam were also allowed to do so. The number of Muslims grew rapidly after that. Mohammad also sent out his emissaries to carry the message of Islam to other countries. In the year 630 CE, Mohammad went to Mecca and many tribes joined him and accepted Islam. The people of Mecca also accepted them. All the idols in the Kaaba were removed.

He made his last Hajj or pilgrimage from Medina to Mecca in 632 CE. In his last sermon there, he asked the people to follow the teachings of the Quran and his own example. Meanwhile, Islam started spreading to other nations. He returned to Medina and passed away in June 632 CE. By then, various Arab tribes had been united into one under Islam.

In his personal life, Mohammad observed all the requirements about prayer and fasting. He prayed often and long, 'till his knees became swollen'. He also fasted several times, including during Ramadan (or Ramzan). He did not sleep much but was always awake early for the morning prayers. He was often moved to tears when praying or when hearing the Quran being recited. He prayed perhaps not for himself but for other people. In one Hadith, it is reported that he prays 'O Allah, it is only You that have promised that when these people make *istighfaar* (repentance and prayers for forgiveness), there will be no punishment.'"

He was also forgiving. During one of the battles, he was resting under a tree when someone called Ghawrath ibn al-Harith threatened Mohammad with a sword and asked mockingly, 'Who will save you?' Without any fear, Mohammad replied 'Allah'. The sword slipped and fell from the assailant's hand. Mohammad took the sword and asked him, 'Who will save you?' The man begged for forgiveness. Mohammad pardoned him and let him go.

He led a simple, austere life. When someone wept at the sight of him lying on a mat of palm leaves, and said that there were those who slept on velvet and silk, Mohammad replied, 'It is not a thing to cry about. For them is the world and for us the hereafter.' In another incident, a woman sent a soft bed for him. He saw it and asked where it came from. When told that some woman had sent it, he insisted on it being returned. He said, 'I swear an oath if I wish Almighty Allah will line up mountains of gold and silver for me.' He meant that he did not need any luxury. He did a lot of the household work himself.

From the age of twenty-five to fifty, he was monogamous. After the passing away of Khadija, in the last thirteen years of his life, he married ten other women. He did not have any children with these later wives, except perhaps with Maria-al-Qibtiyya. Most of them were widows, and he set an example that vulnerable women should be protected and given dignity. He also married two slave women, thus setting them free. Some marriages were to cement relations with non-Islamic warring tribes. It is worth noting that most of the prophets of the Old Testament had more than one wife, and some had concubines as well. This includes Abraham, the patriarch of the three Abrahamic religions, Moses, Jacob, David, Solomon and others.[1]

Mohammad was also humble and asked his followers not to praise him or exalt him, but to treat him as a servant of Allah. At the same time, his character was noble. He was courteous, respected others, and made people who came to meet him feel welcome. In Hadith (330: 5), Ayesha reports, 'It was not in his nature to talk indecently, nor did he engage himself in the use of obscene language. Nor did he shout and talk in the bazaars. He did not avenge a bad deed with a bad one, but forgave it, and thereafter did not even mention it.' When he was injured by a stone in battle, he lost some teeth and his mouth was filled with blood. His followers asked him to curse the person who threw the stone, but instead he prayed to Allah to give the assailant wisdom. He died with almost no property. At the same time, he was very generous. When the ruler of a nearby kingdom sent him camels loaded with gifts, he gave away everything. He said, 'Only then can I be at peace.' If he could not give, he would pray to Allah to fulfil the wish of the one who asked for something. His major decisions and actions were based on the revelations he received.

The Historical Context

Islam arose in the Mecca and Medina region in the seventh century CE. There were several warring tribes. Many of the tribes were nomadic. For instance, Mohammad's foster mother Halima belonged to the nomadic Bedouin tribe who lived in the desert. The majority depended for their livelihood on animal husbandry, using camels, goats and donkeys, horses and mules. Since much of the land was desert, agriculture was a small part of the economy. Mecca became a major centre for trade. Trading made many wealthy in Mecca.

The Kaaba was an ancient religious place. It is said that it was built by Abraham along with his son Ishmael to worship the one true God. However, over time, this deteriorated into idol worship. There were 360 idols there at the time of the Prophet Mohammad's birth. This related to the number of days in one year of the lunar calendar.

Since trading was common, people from other countries also lived there, though in much smaller numbers. Jerusalem, which is about 1,500 km from Mecca, was the place where Christianity and Judaism arose. So there was some knowledge about the other Abrahamic religions, though very few actually followed either Judaism or Christianity. However, there were a few Jews and Christians in the region. There were also some slaves.

People perhaps did not follow a strictly moral life. They drank, gambled and relations between men and women were not regulated by strong codes. Usury and lending money at very high interest rates were prevalent.* Some of the nomadic tribes also occasionally resorted to looting. There were battles between different tribes. Idols of the vanquished were replaced by those of the victor. All this made the young and thoughtful Mohammad sad. Some scholars believe that he fasted and prayed to get guidance on how to help the people of that region. At the same time, there was a tribal culture. It was based on loyalty to the clan and the tribe. They followed the leader of their clan and tribe. The leaders tried to be men of honour and keep their word. There were some women traders, like Khadija, first wife of the Prophet Mohammad. Polygamy was prevalent. It is likely that animal sacrifices to various deities was also

---

* This perhaps led to the Islamic ban on charging interest, which was termed haram or forbidden.

prevalent. Some of the rules of Islam took these conditions into account. Thus animal sacrifices continued but were now offered to Allah. This has a parallel in Judaism, where animal sacrifices were sanctioned—not to the pre-existing gods with idols, but to Yahweh, the one God. Polygamy in Islam was not eliminated, but restricted to four wives, but conditions were also imposed on such marriages. Adultery was strictly forbidden. Islam, in fact, tried to raise the status of women. Lending money for interest, and drinking alcohol was forbidden and declared *haram*.

Mohammad's teachings were a threat to the established order. He forbade idol worship. A small local economy depended on the offerings that people gave to the various gods. The wealthy also derived prestige from some of the existing religious rites. Some of the poor, working class people and slaves embraced Islam, since it treated all as brothers and equals. It was liberating for them. As the influence of Mohammad and Islam grew, it was seen as a threat to the existing order. After the passing away of Mohammad's uncle Abu Talib, a prominent member of the elite Quraysh tribe, the persecution of Muslims increased, and there were attempts to kill Mohammad.

It is interesting to note that the earlier two Abrahamic religions also arose at a time when the people were persecuted. The Jews were enslaved in Egypt and Moses led them to freedom around 1300 BCE. Jesus became a threat to the rabbis of the very religion he was born into,

Judaism. He was crucified in the year 33 CE. Islam came a few centuries later and also faced great persecution in the early days. It took Mohammad about ten years, from 622 CE, when he migrated to Medina, to his passing away in 632 CE, to establish Islam and overcome violent opposition.

The Sacred Texts

The most sacred text is the Quran, revealed to the Prophet Mohammad by Allah through the angel Gabriel. The Prophet started getting revelations or wahy from the year 610 CE, when he was about forty years old, and continued getting them until his passing away in 632 CE. Whenever the Prophet got a revelation, he called some people around him and dictated the words. This was memorized and written down by the *sahabah,* his companions. Some of the notes were scattered among different people, and were said to be written on leather and palm leaves. After his passing away, there was a need to compile them. The first person to lead this effort was Abu Bakr, the first caliph or leader of Islam after Mohammad. He got the Quran written on sheets or *suhuf.* It was written down after carefully checking with those who had memorized it, and with the available records of the sahabah. Abu Bakr passed away two years later and was succeeded as caliph by Umar. After Umar's death, the written version was kept with Hafsa, who was his daughter and also a wife of the Prophet. The next caliph, Uthman, got four knowledgeable scholars to transcribe the original copy and sent copies to various Islamic territories. They replaced any earlier versions that were circulating. Uthman kept a copy in Medina and sent the original back to Hafsa. The process was completed around the year 650 CE, about eighteen years after the passing away of the Prophet.[2] It is believed that the Quran has to be chanted in the original Arabic. Translations cannot be considered the Quran. The Quran has about 6,000 verses called *ayah* (singular) and *ayat* (plural), though some Muslims say there are 6,200. They are arranged into 114 Surahs or chapters, each with a title.

The Hadith is another set of sacred texts, but they are not considered divine in origin. They have records of the acts and sayings of the Prophet from eyewitnesses. They narrate incidents from his life. They also record teachings that have his approval. Different schools of Islam have interpreted them differently. The Hadith also contain the *sunna*, the practices and obligations of Muslims. The Hadith were compiled over a long time. It is usually understood that the Hadith contains the words of the Prophet, while the sunna describes the actions and events of the Prophet's life, along with practices that he approved. In contrast, the Quran contains the words of Allah, and so has the highest status.

Early Islamic History

As mentioned earlier, the early Muslims faced persecution and had to fight several battles. However, Islam had been established as the major religion in the region within the lifetime of the Prophet and the opposition from Mecca had been overcome by 630 CE. Most of the major tribes of Arabia had accepted Islam. There was peace in the region. The Prophet visited neighbouring leaders and kings or sent envoys or wrote to them. He wrote to the leaders of Byzantine (capital Constantinople, now called Istanbul, in Turkey), Oman, Abyssinia (now Ethiopia), Egypt, Bahrain and Persia (now Iran). Some of them accepted Islam, others did not. The first four caliphs after the Prophet, Abu Bakr, Umar, Uthman and Ali, known as 'Rashidun', expanded Islam to several countries. Their reign lasted from 632 CE, the year of the Prophet's passing away, to 661 CE. Some of the tribes refused to accept Abu Bakr as leader and stopped paying *zakat*. They were subdued and brought back to Islam. Abu Bakr died in 634 CE. Umar was the next caliph. One of his daughters was married to the Prophet. Umar was Caliph for about ten years, from 634 CE to 644 CE. He greatly expanded Islam. He was assassinated by a Persian slave in 644 CE.

The next caliph, Uthman, was a son-in-law of the Prophet. He had to face a revolt from within Islam. This led to a split between the Sunni and Shia sects. He greatly expanded Islam into the Levant (parts of Israel, Jordan, Lebanon and Syria), Egypt, Persia (modern-day Iran), Azerbaijan and Armenia. He also conquered parts of Spain, Cyprus, North Africa and even parts of faraway Sindh, now part of Pakistan. He used a combination of concessions and war to expand and consolidate his empire. He was said to be concerned about the poor and a good administrator. He is remembered for the final compilation of the Quran. He noticed some differences in the recitation of the Quran in different regions. To correct this, a final version was produced. However, he faced a revolt in his last years and was killed by rebels in 656 CE.

The last of the Rashidun was Ali, the son-in-law of the Prophet, husband of his daughter Fatima and also his first cousin, being the son of the Prophet's uncle and guardian, Abu Talib. He moved the caliphate from Medina to Kufa in Iraq. There was a demand to avenge the assassination of Uthman. Ali did not want any division within Islam but had to face the first organized internal war between Muslims, called the *fitnah*. Ayesha, one of the Prophet's wives, fought Ali's army. The rebels were defeated. However, more revolts arose and Ali had to fight more wars against fellow Muslims. In 661 CE, he was assassinated. The caliphate was taken over by Muawiya, who had rebelled against Ali. Muawiya then established the Umayyad caliphate.

The first four caliphs are known by the Sunnis as the Rashidun or the rightly guided caliphs. The Shias consider Ali, the fourth caliph, as their first imam, and do not have the concept of the Rashidun. The Quran was compiled during this period. Islam had also spread to various countries and several successful wars had been fought. The early spread of Islam covered parts of Spain in the west all the way to Sindh in Pakistan in the east. They also controlled parts of Sicily, most of the Middle East and large regions in North Africa. The second Persian empire, known as the Sasanian empire, was conquered by the Muslims along with large parts of the Byzantine empire in modern-day Turkey. This was the headquarters of the Christian church in those days. Perhaps decades of warfare between the Persian and Byzantine empires had weakened them, making it easier for the Muslim conquest.

Islam spread by conquest, through trade and also via missionaries. Local people following polytheistic religions were possibly looking for a unifying religion. Islam provided that. Some Christians and Jews also converted. Islam became the fastest growing religion compared to Buddhism and Christianity, the other two proselytizing religions that believed in conversion.

Major Teachings of the Quran

Some of the well-known verses are given here. The five pillars or *arkan* of Islam are said to be *shahadah* or belief in Allah and in the Prophet Mohammad, *salah* or prayer, *zakat* or charity, *sawm* or fasting during Ramzan and *hajj* or pilgrimage to Mecca for those who are able to do so. These five were distilled later, though all of them are mentioned in the Holy Quran. Here, we give those teachings that are related to these, as well as other important teachings and those that are common across other religions. It is to be noted that when a Quranic verse uses the word 'We', it refers to Allah. It is God speaking directly and the Prophet is only telling us what he heard. For instance, 'And assuredly, We have created man and We know what his physical self whispers to him, and We are nearer to him than even his jugular vein' (Surah Qaf, verse 16), refers to Allah saying that He is even closer to a person than their jugular vein.

The first Surah is what the Prophet was reported to have liked.

Chapter 1. Surah Al-Fatiha

1. All praise belongs to Allah, Lord of all the worlds,
2. The Gracious, the Merciful,
3. Master of the Day of Judgement.
4. Thee alone do we worship and Thee alone do we implore for help.
5. Guide us in the right path,
6. The path of those on whom Thou hast bestowed Thy blessings, those who have not incurred Thy displeasure and those who have not gone astray.

The Quranic verses describing Allah are given below:

'There is no God but Allah, the Living, Self-Subsisting and All-Sustaining. He is not overcome by sleep. The heavens and whatsoever is in the earth belong to Him. Who is he that will intercede with Him except by His permission? He knows what is before and behind them; and they understand nothing of His knowledge except what He pleases. His knowledge extends over the heavens and the earth; and the care of them burdens Him not; and He is the High, the Great'(Surah Al-Baqarah, 2-255).

God said to the Prophet, 'Say, "My Lord knows what is spoken in the heaven and the earth. And He is the All-Hearing, the All-Knowing,"' (Surah Al-Anbya 21–5).

'Allah is the Truth, and it is He Who brings the dead to life, and He has power over all things' (Surah Al-Hajj, 22–6).

'Allah is the Light of the heavens and the earth. The similitude of His light is as a lustrous niche, wherein is a lamp. The lamp is in a glass. The glass is as it were a glittering star. It is lit from a blessed tree, an olive, neither of the east nor of the west, whose oil would well-nigh glow forth even though fire touched it not. Light upon light! Allah guides to His light' (Surah Al-Num, 24–35).

In addition to the attributes of Allah in the earlier verses, there are many references to Allah as merciful, all-knowing and wise, and as the creator of heaven and earth.

Everything belongs to him. Allah also judges all people, and punishes those who go against his teachings.

There are several teachings asking Muslims to pray regularly. In the verse below, Allah teaches us how to pray.

'Say, "My Prayer and my sacrifice and my life and my death are all for Allah, the Lord of the worlds"' (Surah Al-Anam, 6–162).

'When My servants ask thee about Me, say: "I am near. I answer the prayer of the supplicant when he prays to Me. So they should hearken to Me and believe in Me, that they may follow the right way"'(Surah Al-Baqarah 2–186).

The above verse or ayah says something significant: 'I am near.' Allah is telling the Prophet to tell the people that He is near.

'And observe Prayer at the two ends of the day, and in the hours of the night that are nearer the day. Surely, good works drive away evil works. This is a reminder for those who would remember'(Surah Hud 11–114).

'Recite that which has been revealed to you from the Book, and observe Prayer. Surely, Prayer restrains one from indecency and manifest evil, and remembrance of Allah indeed is the greatest virtue. And Allah knows what you do' (Surah Al-Ankabut 29–45).

'Observe Prayer, and enjoin good, and forbid evil, and endure patiently whatever may befall thee. Surely this is of those matters which require firm resolve' (Surah Luqman, 31–17).

'O ye who believe! Remember Allah with much remembrance; and glorify Him morning and evening. He it is Who sends blessings on you, as do His angels, that He may bring you forth from all kinds of darkness into light. And He is Merciful to the believers' (Surah al-Ahzab 33-40).

'Allah burdens not any soul beyond its capacity. It shall have the reward it earns, and it shall get the punishment it incurs. Our Lord, do not punish us, if we forget or fall into error; and our Lord, lay not on us a responsibility as Thou didst lay upon those before us. Our Lord, burden us not with what we have not the strength to bear; and efface our sins, and grant us forgiveness and have mercy on us; Thou art our Master[3]' (Surah Al-Baqarah 2–286).

After prayer comes zakat, charity. It is mentioned several times, nearly always along with prayer. There is an obligation to spend some part of one's income for charity, for the poor. Some teachings are also about giving charity as a penance for any wrongdoing. Allah promises that He will purify those who are devoted and do good deeds.

'If you give alms openly, it is well and good; but if you conceal them and give them to the poor, it is better for you; and He will remove from you many of your sins. And Allah is aware of what you do.' (Surah Al-Baqarah, 2–271). The idea that selfless charity purifies is repeated in the next few verses. It says that Allah is pleased with such actions and rewards them.

It also says '. . . but whatever you give in zakat seeking the favour of Allah, it will increase their wealth (or blessings) manifold' (Surah Ar-Rum, 30-39). In Surah Al-Lail, it says, 'Who gives his wealth to become purified, owes no favour to anyone, which is to be repaid. He only gives his wealth to seek the blessings of Allah, who will soon be well pleased with him' (Surah Al-Lail, 92-18-21). Thus, charity done with the purpose of seeking a favour gives worldly rewards, while charity given only for purification pleases Allah.

Fasting during Ramadan is mentioned a few times in the Quran. This is elaborated upon in the Hadith. Hajj is also mentioned in the Quran for those who can afford it, and for those who are not very sick or old or otherwise handicapped.

In addition to these, there are some practical moral teachings. 'O my dear son! observe Prayer, and do good, and avoid evil, and endure patiently whatever may befall you. Surely these matters require firm resolve. Turn not your cheek away from men in pride nor walk on the earth haughtily; surely, Allah loves not any arrogant boaster' (Surah Al-Luqman, 31- 117-19).

'A kind word and forgiveness are better than charity followed by injury. And Allah is Self-Sufficient, Forbearing' (Surah Al-Baqarah, 2–263).

'We have pointed out to him the two ways. But he attempted not the ascent (i.e., ascent for Allah, for a higher or better life). What is the way? It is freeing a slave or feeding a hungry orphan near of kin, or a poor man in need. Again, he should tell those who believe and exhort them to mercy' (Surah Al-Balad, 90 – 10-17). In another Surah it says, 'To him who seeks thy help, turn him not away' (Surah Al-Duah 93-10).

The Quran also teaches us to be humble, charitable, avoid adultery, be trustworthy and prayerful. This helps us reach Allah.

The teachings of the Quran are in different categories. One set reinforces belief in Allah through various verses that mention his mercy, omniscience, power as the Creator and so on. Another set of teachings tells us to pray to Him. There are several references to earlier scriptures, particularly the Torah. Moses, Abraham, Jesus and his mother Mary are mentioned several times. In the Quran Allah also says, 'We make no distinction between any of His Messengers' (Surah Al-Baqarah 2–285). Thus the Quran accepts the Old Testament as well as their prophets. There are also several practical teachings about life, including marriage, property, trade and rituals. Moral and ethical teachings are also given.

Theology

Islam has a well-developed theology about Allah, the Quran and how human beings understand the Quran and

Allah. A central belief is that there is only one God, Allah. He is omnipotent and omniscient, He sees and hears everything, He is Living. He does not have any partners. Idol or image worship is not accepted. Islam accepts the existence of angels and *jinns* or mischievous spirits. The angels are headed by Jibrail (Gabriel), who revealed Allah's words to the Prophet Mohammad.

The Christian idea of the Holy Trinity is not accepted in Islam. They also do not accept Jesus Christ as the Son of God, who acts on behalf of God. Islam says Allah does not have any intermediaries. Jesus in Islam is therefore one of the prophets or messengers of Allah. All the earlier prophets from the Old Testament are accepted as messengers of Allah. The Prophet Mohammad is the last and final prophet. The earlier religions of Judaism and Christianity, which are based on kitab or book, are accepted because Allah spoke to them. At the same time, the Quran is unique among all scriptures because it contains the words of Allah and not of the Prophet Mohammad. Scriptures of other religions contain the teachings of the prophets and not only of Allah. Though the Hadiths are revered, they contain the words of the Prophet Mohammad, and have a lesser status than the Quran. In fact, some scholars classify some of the Hadith as authentic and reject other verses.

Later sects like the Bahais and the Ahmadiyya broke away, claiming that new prophets had emerged, but orthodox Islam remains critical of them.

Islam, like Christianity, believes in the Day of Judgement. Surah 4:136 says, 'Whoever disbelieves in Allah and His angels, and His Books, and His Messengers, and the Last Day, has surely strayed far away.' Human beings will be judged according to their actions and either go to Jannat (paradise) or to Jahannam (hell). One's good deeds must outweigh the bad. Allah decides the fate of each human being on the Day of Judgement.

Over the first few centuries, Islam developed various schools of thought. There are many details and nuances in these philosophies, but only some of the important aspects are given here.

The earliest was the Mu'tazila school founded by Wasil ibn Ata in the early eighth century. The word Mu'tazila literally means those who withdraw. One question was whether Allah and His attributes were separate or not. The Mu'tazila held that they could not be separated. It emphasizes the need to use reason, and says that human beings have free will. This school may have been influenced by Greek philosophy. However, it accepts the core beliefs of Islam, like the Oneness of Allah, the Quran as the words of Allah and the Prophet Mohammad as a messenger of Allah. They say that Allah created the Quran, which other sects reject, saying that the Quran is not created but always existed. Evil was the outcome of man's free will and not created by Allah. Human intelligence can understand what is good and evil.

Soon after that, the Athari school developed. They were part of the Sunni sect of Islam. They said that all interpretation of the Quran needs to be avoided. The texts have to be understood literally as they are. They also included some of the Hadiths in their doctrine.

There was a reaction to these extremes. The most prominent was from the mainstream Sunni establishment. The earliest were the Ashari. They said that revelation is higher than reason. The Quran contains revelations and reason cannot judge what is contained in it. They separated the essence of Allah and His attributes, but said that the latter had no separate reality.* Good and evil are what Allah commands in the Quran, and that is not to be judged by human reason. Free will is also given by Allah, and is limited to deciding between what Allah has created. Individuals, therefore, bear responsibility for their actions, though behind all this Allah controls and decides everything. The Quran is uncreated and always existed, though the sounds and words came into being later. The Ashari doctrine has the largest number of adherents today.

Each of these schools added more books written by scholars who further developed these doctrines. Other

---

* There are such debates even in Hindu philosophy. For instance, Advaita says reality is one and the attributes of that reality are either illusory or cannot be separated from it. Visishtadvaita, on the other hand, says that reality or God is qualified by its attributes.

schools of thought like the Maturidi also emerged within the Sunni sect.

Spiritual and Mystical Traditions in Islam

In a sense, the mystical tradition begins with the Quran itself. These are the revelations that the Prophet Mohammad got from Allah through the angel Gabriel.

However, if we probe further, there are references to what many consider mystical. There are 114 Suras, of which twenty-nine begin with some syllables. These are Alif-Lal-Meem, Alif-Lal-Meem-Sad, Alif-Lal-Ra and so on. Scholars differ on what they mean. Some say that only Allah knows what it means. For them, this is proof that the Prophet did not create the Quran, but that it came from Allah, as these syllables have no meaning we can understand. Other scholars give a meaning to them. Some say these refers to the *noor* or Light of Allah. Others like Ibn Abbas say it means 'I am Allah, the All Knowing.' [3]

There is a reference to the soul: 'He indeed truly prospers who purifies it' (the soul) (Surah 91-9).[*] Allah says, 'We are nearer to him than even his jugular vein' (Surah 50:16). In Surah 2:115, it is said '. . . wherever you turn, there will be the face of Allah.' Two of the

---

[*] 'Blessed are the pure in heart, for they shall see God' (Mathew 5:8, Sermon on the Mount) is very similar.

essential elements of mysticism—that the divine is in the soul, and that God is everywhere, are mentioned in these two previous verses of the Quran. There are several verses that say that Allah breathed his spirit into human beings (Surahs 3:49; 5:39; 15:29; 32:9; 38:72).* 4

The Sufi tradition emphasizes the mystical aspect of Islam and says that the Quran is the basis of their doctrines. The Sufi's quest is union of the individual soul with Allah, which leads to joy. A central aspect of the teaching is constantly remembering Allah. The Quran has verses asking us to remember Him. 'And remember thy Lord much . . .' (Surah 3:41), 'O ye who believe! remember Allah with much remembrance' (Surah 33:41), 'The heart finds rest in Allah's remembrance' (Surah 13:28).

Sufism is also called *tasawuff* (dressing in wool) as the early practitioners performed this type of austerity. They lived a life of poverty and are called fakirs or dervishes. Sufism tries to find God through direct experience. This was true of the Essenes in the Judaic tradition as well as of the Desert Fathers who emerged soon after Christ. Sufism emphasizes love of Allah. Through this love, the aspirant tries to eventually experience Allah. The term used is *tawwakul* or absolute reliance on Allah. There is a system of teacher and disciple. The student follows the

---

* There are references to the Holy Spirit, also called ruah, in the Old Testament and in the Christian Gospels.

instructions of the teacher, who guides them towards the experience of Allah.

Some of the well-known Sufi masters were Ibn al' Arabi and Ibn al-Farid, who wrote in Arabic, and Farid al-Din Attar and Jalal al-Din al-Rumi, who wrote in Persian. Over time, various philosophers and sects emerged among the Sufis. For instance, one group said there was unity of existence, meaning that the human soul could finally merge with Allah. One famous Sufi who said 'Anal Haq' or 'I am the Truth' was Mansur Al-Hallaj. Rabia Basri, a woman, was an early Sufi saint who is still revered. She said that one must love God for His own sake and not for gaining paradise or out of fear of going to hell.

Other schools of thought that differed from the *wahdat al-wujūd* (unity of existence) philosophy emerged. Another called *wahdat al-shuhūd* (unity of vision) said it was a subjective experience and could not be objectified. In all cases, the final goal is *fana* or submergence of one's identity with Allah.

All the various sects accept the Quran and the Prophet Mohammad. They interpret the Quran at an inner or esoteric level and emphasize some verses there like 'And remember Allah often' (Surah 62:10). They emphasize verses of the Quran that describe the divine as immanent or within the human soul. The Sufi philosophy says that this divinity can be experienced. Surah 2:109 says, 'Wherever you turn, there will be the face of Allah' and Surah 50:16 says, 'Allah is closer to you than your jugular vein.'

Such mystics were not always accepted by the mainstream religion. Some of their teachings were considered blasphemous. The idea of a student going to a teacher was said to be against the Quran, which did not accept intermediaries like idols or images between the human being and Allah. The Sufis also refer to Hadith verses like 'Neither My Earth nor My Heavens could contain Me, whilst the heart of My believing servant does contain Me.' (Hadith 5). Mainstream Islam either rejects the Hadith as inauthentic or interprets it to say that the human heart can have love of Allah but He does not reside there. At the same time, the Sufis did have a following among the people and perhaps continue to do so.[5]

At a philosophical level, the different sects of Sufism all say that Allah is immanent, that He can be experienced, and that love is the means of experiencing the divine. Some sects say that leads to fana or complete annihilation or submission of the ego to Allah. Some say this leads to a complete merger with the divine. They refer to Quranic verses like 'All things in creation will pass away (be annihilated) and there remains only the Lord in majesty and honour' (Surah 55:26–27).

The philosophy and interpretation of the Sufis is rejected by most of the mainstream scholars and preachers of Islam. They say Allah is not immanent in the human soul, and that our duty is to follow His teachings as laid down in the Quran.

Sects in Islam

Like other great religions, Islam also split first into two, Sunni and Shia, and later into various other sects. Another early offshoot called the Kharijites emerged during the first internal war in Islam in 656-661 CE. However, they are not active today. The Sunnis are by far the largest group in Islam and comprise well over 80 per cent of the Islamic population in the world. The Shias are largely confined to modern-day Iran and are a majority in other countries like Iraq, Bahrain and Azerbaijan. The major split was about the proper successor to the Prophet Mohammad. The Sunnis say that Abu Bakr and the next three caliphs were the true successors of the Prophet. They were the Rashidun or rightly guided caliphs. The Shias, on the other hand, say that the fourth caliph, Ali, who was also a cousin and son-in-law of the Prophet, was the true successor to the Prophet.

Even among the Sunnis, various branches holding slightly different beliefs emerged between the eighth and ninth centuries CE. These include the Hanafi, Maliki, Shafi, Hanbali and Zahiri schools. If the Quran or the Sharia (derived from the Quran and the Hadiths) did not lay down clear procedures, there was the possibility of disputes arising. There was a need to have common laws or a basis or methodology for deriving such laws and regulations. Similarly, within the Shias also, there are different branches. Various reform movements also came about later. However, all accept the five pillars of Islam, including the Quran and the Prophet Mohammad.

The Shia sect gave rise to the Nusayrites or Alawites and Yazdis. The Bohra Muslims are another prominent sect in Islam and are considered to be part of Shi'ism. The Nizari Ismā'īli Shias headed by the Aga Khan is a prominent modern sect. Their leader or Imam claims direct descent from the Prophet Mohammad.

Later, the Bahais emerged and declared themselves independent of Islam. The Sufis, with various denominations, are also sects within Islam which emphasize a mystical approach to Allah. In the latter half of the nineteenth century, the Ahmadiyya sect emerged from Punjab in India.

Notes

Islam emerged when the other Abrahamic religions were already established. In the early days, the religion was confined to the regions around Mecca, where the dominant religion was polytheistic. However, there were a few Christians and Jews as well. As Islam spread to other countries over the next few centuries, contact with

Christianity increased. Christian theology was already well-developed. In the intellectual domain, there was greater familiarity with Greek philosophy. Islamic theology positioned itself among these pre-existing doctrines.

Islam includes not only theology, but also jurisprudence and ethics. Jurisprudence is derived from the Quran and the Hadiths. It is also known as the Sharia. It gives teachings about everyday life, trade, treatment of family members, marriage, slaves and so on. In common with Christianity, it believes in the Day of Judgement, and eternal heaven or hell. Judaism is silent on this issue.

According to historians, a majority of the people in Mecca at the time of the Prophet were not literate. This was true at the time of Moses and Jesus also. The contents of the Quran are simple and easy to understand, though some of the Sufis and others said they could be interpreted at different levels. However, over time, Islam probably helped to spread literacy as well because of the need to read and recite the Quran. Scholars and historians speak of the Golden Age of Islam. If we focus only on the cultural, scientific and mathematical developments, they were probably at their peak in the period from about 850 CE to the time of the Crusades, around 1100 CE. During this time, art, poetry, philosophy, mathematics and science flourished. Various Quranic verses about knowledge may have led to more people becoming literate. There was a period where Greek philosophy was studied and translated. But there was a lot of original work being produced as well.

Jerusalem, sacred earlier to Jews and Christians, became sacred to Islam after Mohammad's revelation of the winged horse. As early as 638 CE, a few years after the Prophet passed away, Jerusalem first came under Islamic rule under the second Rashidun caliph, Umar.

THE INDIAN RELIGIONS

BUDDHISM, JAINISM,
SIKHISM AND HINDUISM

INTRODUCTION TO THE
INDIAN RELIGIONS

Four of the world's religions that exist today and have written sacred texts arose in India. The most ancient is Hinduism, older even than Judaism. Jainism and Buddhism are contemporary, although Jainism may have slightly predated Buddhism. The last religion with a significant following is Sikhism, which arose in the sixteenth century.

The three ancient religions of India did not face persecution like the Abrahamic religions. Sikhism did face persecution after a few decades from the political powers that ruled India at that time. The focus of these religions was spiritual. The practical life is not neglected, but the highest regard has been for the spiritual life.

They all share a common belief in reincarnation and eventual release from birth and death, termed liberation. There is no concept of eternal heaven and hell. Hinduism is not based on any founder but on the sacred texts, the

Vedas, the Upanishads and the Bhagavad Gita. The other three religions are based on a founder or set of founders. Only Buddhism is a proselytizing religion, and within a few centuries of its origin, it dominated Indian religion. A majority of Indians were Buddhist. However, over the centuries, Buddhism declined in India, though it continues in various other Asian countries. The other three religions are non-proselytizing. Their numbers have not grown significantly over time except by natural growth in population. Hinduism continues to be the majority religion in India.

Jainism is atheistic and Buddhism is agnostic about God. Sikhism is explicitly theist, though it does not accept idol worship. They consider their sacred text as their teacher or guru. In practice, Jainism has temples with idols of their most revered teachers, called the Tirthankaras. However, they are not considered gods. Many Buddhist temples also have images of Buddha. Hinduism is the only world religion that accepts idol worship.

Like all religions, the Indian religions also split into various sects. Hinduism in a sense was never a unified religion, and developed innumerable sects over the centuries. Buddhism, Jainism and Hinduism have highly developed philosophies with dozens of books written over the millennia. Some of them refuted the doctrines of other religions. These doctrinal differences were present even within a religion, most notably in Hinduism. The Indian religions exist in peace with each other today, though there are historic records of conflict. However, these differences never gave rise to war.

4

BUDDHISM

A Short Life History of Buddha

Buddhism was founded by Gautama Siddhartha. After illumination, he was called Buddha. He is also referred to as Sakyamuni, Tathagata and the Blessed One. The exact dates of his life are not known with certainty. But there is some consensus that he was born in 563 BCE and passed away in 483 BCE. He attained illumination at the age of about thirty-six and preached for forty four years till his final passing away. He was born into a princely family in Lumbini, a small town in present-day Nepal near the border with India. His father Suddhodana was the ruler of a small kingdom. His mother Maya conceived him when, in a vision, a white elephant entered her right side. His mother died at childbirth and he was brought up by her sister, Mahaprajapati, who became his foster mother.

At the age of sixteen, Siddhartha was married to Yashoda. They had a son called Rahul. At the age of twenty-nine, Siddhartha left home and became a wandering monk. He visited various teachers and practiced different methods of austerity to gain enlightenment. After some years, he decided to fall back on his own efforts. He sat under a banyan tree with a firm resolve, saying to himself, 'Let my bones rot, but I will not get up till I get illumination.' He was illumined and it is said that he remained in that state for eighty days. The sacred banyan tree in Bodh Gaya in present-day Bihar in India is believed to be the same one under which Buddha got enlightenment.*

His teaching and ministry started after that. He came to Sarnath near Varanasi, where his first recorded teaching is available. This was the sermon on the Four Noble Truths, and is the basis of Buddhism. Over the years, several people became his disciples, and kings also accepted him as their teacher. Buddha passed away in Kushinagar in the present-day state of Uttar Pradesh in India. It is believed in India that Buddha was born, attained enlightenment and passed away on a full moon night, called Buddha Purnima. However, the belief varies in different countries.

---

* Also believed that a sapling from the original tree was taken to Sri Lanka, and a sapling from that brought back when the original tree in Bodh Gaya withered away.

Some Incidents from the Life of Buddha

Angulimala had vowed to kill 1,000 persons and make a garland of the fingers of the dead. The word *anguli* means finger, and *mala* means garland. He had already killed 999 people and was waiting for one more to complete his tally. Buddha met him in the forest all alone. Though Angulimala came to kill him, Buddha subdued him with his calm presence, and in fact converted him into a monk when Angulimala repented. It is said that he finally gained enlightenment. This story illustrates that no matter what sins we may have committed, we can be redeemed if we want to be. Angulimala, however, had to suffer the consequences of his evil actions before attaining Nirvana.

The Sacred Texts

Buddha's teachings were recorded by his disciples. A few decades after his passing away, the first Buddhist conclave was held in Rajgir in Bihar. This was supported by the king at the time. Buddha's chief disciple, Ananda, came forward and recited the teachings. These were accepted and formed the Sutta* Pitaka or the Sutra Basket of teachings. This is considered Buddhavachana or words of

---

* Sutta in the Pali language used by Buddha is derived from the Sanskrit word Sutra, which means teachings in this context. Many Pali words are simplified forms of Sanskrit words.

Buddha by the Theravada sect of Buddhism. The well-known Dhammapada is part of this text. Another disciple, Upali, came forward and recited the Vinaya Pitaka, which are the rules for monks. This was derived from the words and teachings of Buddha but are not considered the original words of Buddha. A hundred or more years later, the Abhidhamma Pitaka was written down. This puts the teachings of Buddha into a philosophical framework and explains them. It was written by later scholars. Together, the Vinaya, Sutta and Abhidhamma Pitakas form the Tripitakas (three baskets) that contain the core teachings of the Theravada sect of Buddhism.

Over the centuries, several other great scholars added to the wealth of Buddhist literature, including Buddhaghosha, Nagarjuna and several Chinese and South-east Asian scholars. Buddhism later split into the Theravada, Mahayana and Vajrayana schools. Theravada prevails in Sri Lanka, where the original Pali canon was written down, and in South-east Asia. The Mahayana remained for several centuries in several parts of India and is also prevalent in East Asia, including in China. The Vajrayana arose in Tibet. The Madhyamaka and Yogachara philosophies evolved out of Mahayana. Zen, another well-known philosophy, also evolved from the Mahayana traditions prevalent in China. Shunyavada or the doctrine of emptiness also came out of Mahayana and is attributed to Nagarjuna. One apparently major doctrinal difference between Mahayana and the other schools is the concept of the *boddhisattva*. Mahayana holds up the ideal of a spiritual seeker who foregoes ultimate Nirvana or release from birth and death and chooses rebirth so that he can help others who are not yet enlightened. Such a one is the bodhisattva. Theravada rejects this notion and says Buddha said Nirvana is the goal of life and that each one has to work out his own salvation. Several scholarly debates took place between the sects as well as with Hindu philosophers over the centuries. The Vajrayana sect incorporates tantric practices and is also called Mantrayana. It includes chanting of mantras and several esoteric practices.

In many religions, the words of the founder are sometimes lost in the wealth of literature, rituals and philosophies that came later. However, all the Buddhist schools accept the words of Buddha as final. In particular, they all accept the Four Noble Truths and the Eight Fold Path taught by Buddha.

Some Preliminaries

Buddhism accepts the theory of rebirth. Karma or action done with desire leads to *sankhara* (Sanskrit *samskara*) or impressions in the mind. These impressions lead to further action, which in turn causes further impressions. This leads to rebirth for the purpose of reaping the results of karma. *Tanha* or clinging to anything impermanent leads to the endless cycle of karma and rebirth. Though such clinging or attachment may give temporary happiness, it eventually leads to suffering. The word *dukkha* or suffering is repeatedly used. These precepts are common to other Indian religions. The themes of love, kindness and compassion, and giving up hatred, greed and selfishness, are also repeatedly emphasized.

Important Teachings

The principal text from which this is drawn is the Sutta Pitaka. The Dhammapada is in the Khuddaka Nikaya or the fifth and final section of the Sutta Pitaka. It is the most widely known text, reputed to be the distilled words of Buddha.

The Sutta Pitaka contains Buddha's teachings spread over four and a half decades from the age of thirty six to the age of eighty. The discourses were meant for earnest seekers. They also contain sections with questions and answers. Sometimes the questions are posed by Buddha himself to the student or disciple. It does not have detailed discussions about the origin of the universe, about the nature of God and about man's relationship with the universe or God. It does have statements showing that such questions are not very important for the earnest seeker who wants to lead a better life or seek Nirvana.

The original words of Buddha are in Pali, a language that is no longer spoken today. However, many scholars and monks have studied Pali and provided translations. Pali is derived from Sanskrit and we can understand the meaning from the context and sometimes from its Sanskrit root. It is likely that Buddha knew Pali, Prakrit, Sanskrit and some of the local dialects of that time. But he preached in the language of the people and not in Sanskrit, which was known only to a select few.

The Four Noble Truths

The Four Noble Truths are the basis of Buddha's teachings. He taught it several times over the years. The first time was in Sarnath to his first five disciples. There are various versions of the original Pali texts. One of them is given below.

1. **Dukkhaṁ Ariyasaccaṁ**
   The Noble Truth of Suffering
2. **Dukkhasamudayaṁ Ariyasaccaṁ**
   The Noble Truth of the Arising of Suffering
3. **Dukkhanirodhaṁ Ariyasaccaṁ**
   The Noble Truth of the Cessation of Suffering
4. **Dukkhanirodhagāmanī Paṭipadā Ariyasaccaṁ**
   The Noble Truth of the Practice Leading to the Cessation of Suffering

The word dukkha occurs in all the four Truths. It is usually translated as suffering. Others have understood it to mean feelings of dissatisfaction, the fact that nothing is permanent, that the joys we experience are fleeting and so on. There is a subconscious feeling that there is no permanent peace or joy, that one is never completely happy. The word *saccam* is derived from Sanskrit *satyam* and means truth. Whatever the translation, the first Noble Truth says that dukkha is a noble (*ariya*) truth (saccam). This is something that everyone experiences. It does not refer to any mystical revelation.

It explains in more detail that birth, old age and death are suffering, that grief, pain, sorrow and despair are suffering. Not obtaining what one desires is also suffering.

The second Noble Truth uses the word *Dukkhasamudayam*. In Pali, the word *samudayam* means origin. It means there is an origin or cause of suffering. This assumes that if we experience or perceive something, it has an origin or cause. Desire, craving, ignorance are all causes of suffering. Here, ignorance refers to not knowing that actions done with desire lead eventually to suffering. Attachment to the senses leads to actions that cause suffering. Some versions use three words, *kamatanha, bhavatanha* and *vibhavatanha*. Tanha means craving or clinging. Kamatanha is craving for pleasure, bhavatanha is craving for the continuation or recurrence of pleasure and vibhavatanha is the craving for ending unpleasant experiences. The second Noble Truth says that by craving or clinging to that which is impermanent, we continue to suffer. Anything that changes or is impermanent cannot lead to permanent joy.

The third Noble Truth uses the word *Dukkhanirodhaṁ*. *Nirodha* in Sanskrit and Pali means control or removal. The third truth is that suffering can cease. The logical connection is clear: if there is a cause of suffering, then removing that cause will lead to an end of suffering. Cessation of all craving ends suffering. The famous words Buddha uses while addressing the monks are *taṇhāya asesavirāganirodho cāgo paṭinissaggo mutti anālayo*. A simple translation is: (through) a complete cessation of craving, by giving up, by forsaking (the impermanent), you get freedom and release from all attachments.* The end of suffering leads to *mutti* (Sanskrit *mukti*), meaning release and freedom. This means Nirvana.

The fourth Noble Truth uses the words *Dukkhanirodhagāmanī patipada*. Nirodha means cessation in this context, *agamani* means coming again or recurrence and *patipada* is the way or method of ending all suffering. The fourth Noble Truth gives the method for removing suffering. This method is the well-known Eight Fold Path. The eight steps all use the word *samma*, usually translated

---

* A word by word translation is *tanha* or craving, *asesa,* without any residue, complete, *virag,* absence of attraction or desire, *cago* (from Sanskrit tyaga, renunciation or giving up), *patinissago* (from Sanskrit *pratinihsarga*) or abandonment (of all cravings), *mutti* (from Sanskrit mukti), freedom, *analayo,* freedom from attachment

to mean right. Thus, the first one is *samma ditti* or right view. Ditti comes from the Sanskrit word *drishti*, meaning sight. Another translation of samma is complete or whole. So it means 'complete or wholesome view'.

Since the Eight Fold Path has been explained in various other texts, only a brief summary is given here. The eight steps are related to view, thought or aspiration or will, speech, action, way of life, effort, mindfulness and samadhi or complete absorption of the mind. In the first step, samma ditti, we have to understand and view things correctly. If we understand that there is no permanent joy in our everyday life, or that everything is changing and impermanent or that everything is suffering, we no longer hanker for such things.

This leads to the second step, *samma sankalpa* or right thought or aspiration. The aspirant's thoughts have to be free of sensuous hankerings, ill will and cruelty. Some scholars interpret sankalpa to mean the aspiration to remove all suffering. *Samma vacha* or right speech is abstaining from lying, harsh language and vain talk. Right speech also means truthful, mild and wise words. *Samma kammanta* or right (bodily) action means abstaining from killing, stealing and sexual misconduct. *Sammajiva* or right livelihood means giving up lying and deceit for obtaining one's livelihood. *Samma vāyāma* or right effort is control over the mind. It says negative thoughts should not be entertained, and should not be allowed to arise. It also means that the mind must be kept on positive and wholesome thoughts. *Samma sati* is right mindfulness. It asks us to be aware.

These are the preparatory steps for the last step. Control of the mind is possible with right understanding, control of thoughts and desires, and following moral precepts that help calm the mind.

Samma samadhi is the final step in the Eight Fold Path. Buddha describes four stages. In the first stage, the mind is calm and undisturbed, there is one thought to the exclusion of everything else and it leads to rapture and joy. In the second stage, the thought is also gone and the mind enters greater joy and peace. In the next stage, the aspirant goes beyond the rapture and becomes equanimous and fully conscious. In the final stage, the aspirant goes beyond pleasure and pain and attains Nirvana. In another context, Nirvana is also said to be ego-lessness. Practice of the Eight Fold Path ultimately leads to Nirvana.[1]

The basis of Buddhism, the Four Noble Truths, is practical and not metaphysical, philosophical or even religious. There is a background to it which was known to those who heard it. It is the law of karma or of action. It says that every action has a consequence that we experience. This leads to sankhara or impressions in the mind, which creates attachment, aversion and craving. Thus, the second truth says that craving pleasure, wanting to continue it and avoid unpleasant things, creates thought patterns or impressions. The third truth says that by giving up desire, attachment and clinging to impermanent things, these impressions are finally removed, leading to release or liberation.

Buddha knew very well that this was easier said than done. He says that without experiencing the results of our actions, we cannot put an end to suffering. So he taught the Eight Fold Path.

Other Essential Teachings from the Sutta Pitaka

Buddha says that there are four things that no one can change. That which is subject to decay will eventually decay. That which is subject to illness will fall ill. That which is subject to death will die. All actions done with desire will lead to rebirth. To add emphasis, he says no ascetic, brahmin, heavenly being, god, devil or anyone in this world can change these four things. He is emphasizing that there is no permanent peace or joy here. He says that corporeality or identification with the body, feeling, thoughts and what we perceive through our senses are all impermanent. We should therefore not identify with them. This eventually leads to liberation.

We have to experience the results of both good and evil actions. Greed, hate and delusion are great barriers to Nirvana. Those who can give these up are close to Nirvana in this very life.

The end of suffering is logically explained. First, ignorance or *avijja* (Sanskrit *avidya*) is the root cause. By overcoming ignorance, formation of further binding impressions or sankhara eventually cease. We cling to impermanent things out of ignorance, which leads to suffering. Once we overcome that, it leads to the cessation of the constant turmoil in the mind and attachment to the world of name and form. It then leads to the cessation of the constant pull of the sense organs and the mind, which then leads to the cessation of the impressions in the mind that trouble us. This leads to the removal of craving and clinging, leading to the cessation of binding karma and rebirth. This removes suffering due to old age, grief, pain and despair. It leads to a complete cessation of all suffering, which is Nirvana.

The source of craving or tanha is explained. It first arises from feeling. Feelings arise from contact with the senses, which are activated by *nama rupa* or name and form, which are perceived through consciousness, *viññāṇa*. Consciousness arises from the deeper impressions sankhara, which arise from ignorance avijja.* Thus, ignorance is the root cause of our craving, which eventually leads to suffering.

---

* *Vinnana* comes from the Sanskrit word *vijnana*. Here it refers to the consciousness through which sensory objects are perceived. In Hinduism Vijnana means something else and refers to deeper wisdom.

Elsewhere, Buddha describes the state of Nibbana (Sanskrit Nirvana). It is full of peace, sublime, the end of all karma and formations of impressions in the mind, and the removal of all craving. No thought of 'I' and 'mine' arise. In another place, *anatta* or annihilation of the ego is described as Nirvana. He says that one who is close to achieving this may see extraordinary or sublime visions, hear sounds, smell things and so on, but nothing can disturb them as they know that even these are impermanent.

An enlightened person is filled with love and is free of the thirsting after life and its pleasures; their mind is freed from the senses, their heart is still, they do not add to their karma and there remains nothing for them to do.

Exalted Utterances

Buddha also describes the state of Nirvana in poetic terms. In the Udana or exalted utterances of the Khuddaka Nikaya of the Sutta Pitaka, there are several utterances of Buddha. Some of them are given below.

In the Bahiyasuttam or discourse on Bahiya, a monk, Buddha says:

'*Yattha āpo ca paṭhavī, tejo vāyo na gādhati,*
Na tattha sukkā jotanti, ādicco nappakāsati,
Na tattha candimā bhāti, tamo tattha na vijjati.

Yadā ca attanā vedī, muni monena brāhmaṇo,
Atha rūpā arūpā ca, sukhadukkhā pamuccatī'.

'Where there is no water, earth, fire and wind, where the stars do not shine, nor does the sun—there the moon does not shine, and there is no darkness. When the sage, the brāhmaṇa, has experienced it, then he is free from both form and formless, happiness and suffering.'

The Udānavarga (Nirvāṇavarga 26-24, 25) says,

'Abhijānāmy ahaṁ sthānaṁ yatra bhūtaṁ na vidyate.
Nākāśaṁ na ca vijñānaṁ, na sūryaś candramā na ca;
Naivāgatir na ca gatir, nopapattiś cyutir na ca.
Apratiṣṭham anālambaṁ - duḥkhāntaḥ sa nirucyate.'

'That place where the elements are not found I know. There is neither space nor consciousness, no sun nor moon; no coming, no going, no rebirth, no passing away. It is without support or object—this is called the end of suffering.'

Emphasizing that there is indeed a final release, he gives words of assurance in Tatiyanibbānasuttaṁ 8-3 or third discourse on Nirvana:

'Atthi bhikkhave ajātaṁ abhūtaṁ akataṁ asaṅkhataṁ
No ce taṁ bhikkhave abhavissā ajātaṁ abhūtaṁ
akataṁ asaṅkhataṁ, na-y-idha jātassa bhūtassa

katassa saṅkhatassa nissaraṇaṁ paññāyetha.
Yasmā ca kho bhikkhave atthi ajātaṁ abhūtaṁ
akataṁ asaṅkhataṁ, tasmā jātassa bhūtassa
katassa saṅkhatassa nissaraṇaṁ paññāyatī'

'There is, monks, an unborn, unbecome, unmade, unconditioned. If, monks, there were not that unborn, unbecome, unmade, unconditioned, you could not know an escape here from the born, become, made and conditioned. But because there is an unborn, unbecome, unmade, unconditioned, therefore you do know an escape from the born, become, made and conditioned.'

In the Udānavarga (Nirvāṇavarga, 26-21) Buddha says,

'Ajāte sati jātasya vaden niḥsaraṇaṁ sadā.
Asaṁskṛtaṁ ca sampaśyaṁ saṁskṛtāt parimucyate.'

'(Because) there is an unborn, there is always an escape from the born. Seeing the unconditioned he is freed from the conditioned.'

He describes Nirvana as *'susukhaṁ vata taṁ Nibbānaṁ'*, full of joy.

Practical Teachings

In the Udana, Raja suttam, 5:1, he says,

> *Sabbā disā anuparigamma cetasā,*
> *Nevajjhagā piyataram-attanā kvaci.*
> *Evaṁ piyo puthu attā paresaṁ,*
> *Tasmā na hiṁse param-attakāmo'.*

'Having gone around in all directions with the mind, there is surely no one found who is loved more than oneself. In the same way others love themselves, therefore one who cares for himself should not harm another.'

He tells us how to progress on the path in Kolita Sutta 3:5:

> *Sati kāyagatā upaṭṭhitā,*
> *Chasu phassāyatanesu saṁvuto,*
> *Satataṁ bhikkhu samāhito,*
> *Jaññā nibbānam-attano.'*

'Attending to mindfulness related to the body, restrained in regard to the six spheres of contact, the monk who is continually concentrated, can know Nibbāna for himself.' This teaching is simple and straightforward. It says that the aspirant should be mindful of his body and have control over the 'six spheres of contact', i.e., sight, hearing, smell, taste, touch and the mind. Control over the senses and the mind leads to Nirvana.

He describes an ideal monk in Pilindivaccha suttaṁ 3:6:

'Yamhi na māyā vasati na māno,
Yo vītalobho amamo nirāso,
Panunnakodho abhinibbutatto
So brāhmaṇo so samaṇo sa bhikkhu'

'In whom dwells no deceit and no conceit, he who is free from lust, is unselfish and without yearning, who has dispelled anger, who is himself completely emancipated, he is a brāhmaṇa, he is an ascetic, he is a monk.'

Buddha gives a lot of importance to mindfulness. He asks us to be conscious while going and coming; while looking forward and backward; while bending forward and stretching; while eating, drinking, chewing and tasting; while discharging excrement and urine; while walking, standing, sitting, falling asleep and awakening; while speaking and keeping silent. The teaching simply says, always be aware and mindful.

Some Famous Sayings of the Buddha

'Caratha bhikkhave cārikaṁ
bahujana-hitāya bahujana-sukhāya,
lokānukampāya,
atthāya hitāya sukhāya
devamanussānaṁ.'

—Saṁyutta Nikāya, 4.5

Go forth oh monks, for the welfare and happiness of all, out of compassion for the world, for the good, and happiness of gods and men. In particular, the phrase '*bahujana-hitāya bahujana-sukhāya*', meaning 'for the welfare and happiness of all', is used even today.

Buddha, in the Saṃyutta Nikāya 3:8, teaches that just as we love ourselves above all others, so too do others love themselves. Therefore, we should refrain from causing harm to anyone*. He further emphasizes that our minds should remain undisturbed, free of evil thoughts, and our hearts should be filled with love, devoid of any hidden malice.

He also says that even if robbers were to cut off our limbs, our heart should remain full of love and free from any hidden malice. In the Angasutra Nikaya verse 5:16, he says even for a person against whom hatred might arise, one should have love.* These teachings of Buddha are reminiscent of the teachings of all great religions.

In the Hymn of Love in the Sutta Nipata of the Khuddaka Nikaya of the Sutta Pitaka, Buddha says we should never hurt anyone, hate anyone or wish harm on anyone. Just as a mother loves her child, in the same way we should have kindness for all living beings. He further says

---

* Christ says 'Forgive thy enemy, pray for them that curse you.' — Mathew 5:43-48

that the heart is liberated by this all-embracing kindness far more than by any other worldly meritorious act.

Buddha also teaches the middle path, which avoids both sensual indulgence and extreme austerity.* He says that sensual indulgence is unholy and vulgar. He also condemns self-mortification and says that the middle path is suitable. He says that the one whose mind is still is a sage. Other religions say the same.

Buddha also says we should not go by hearsay, tradition, rumours or the texts handed down. He also says we should not believe a thing because it agrees with our fancies and speculations. This is a famous teaching of Buddha. He is not condemning the traditions or the texts. He is also not giving free licence to our whims and fancies. He is telling us to explore something for ourselves and only then accept it.

In his last days, Sariputta, one of his close monk disciples, tells Buddha that he is the greatest teacher that ever was and that there will be none such in the future. Buddha asks him whether Sariputta knows the wisdom of the past enlightened ones, of the future ones or even about the present ones. Sariputta says he does not know. Buddha explicitly says that there were fully enlightened souls in the past, and that there would be more in the future. He does not give himself any special status.

---

* In the Bhagavad Gita, Krishna also asks Arjuna to follow the middle path.

He does not teach that faith by itself will emancipate anyone. He asks people to follow the teachings, strive with energy and thus become free.

Buddha on God and Metaphysics

In the Sangarava Sutta of the Samyutta Nikaya of the Sutta Pitaka, Sangarava, a student, asks Buddha whether the gods exist. Buddha affirms three times that there are gods. Here, the gods do not refer to any being who is the creator, sustainer and lord of the Universe. It refers to celestial beings. Scholars interpret these statements in different ways. One is that these are celestial beings or devas, and they too are subject to death, though they live long. However, seeing such gods or disputing whether they exist or not is irrelevant for one's life here and now. Some say he was being sarcastic. Other scholars say that the question is not important for obtaining Nirvana. Some others say that Buddha did not want to confuse the student because he already believed in something.

There are long passages about Sakka, the king of the gods, who comes with a retinue of thirty-three gods to learn from Buddha. Scholars point out that Sakka is Sakra in Sanskrit, which is another name for Indra, the king of the Hindu gods. There are other references to celestial beings. However, it is clear that Buddha's teachings for both monks and laypersons do not give importance to such gods. It is interesting to note that such gods always pay homage to Buddha.

In the Digha Nikaya or 'Long Discourses' of the Sutta Pitaka, there is a well-known teaching given to two brahmin students. They were arguing about the right method of knowing 'Brahma', the creator (it is not clear whether they refer to the Puranic god of Hinduism, who is said to be the creator, or to 'Brahman', the formless, transcendental reality of Hinduism).

Buddha establishes that their dispute is about the path they should follow since one teacher prescribes one way, and another prescribes a different way. Buddha asks if either of their teachers had seen Brahma, or earlier teachers for seven generations had seen Brahma. The students say that they had not. Buddha says that one who has not seen Brahma cannot teach someone else how to see him. He also says that the teachers were attached to their senses and such people can never know Brahma.

He then establishes that the senior, elder teachers say that Brahma is not possessive (or greedy), has no enmity, has no ill will, has a pure heart and is powerful. He tells them to cultivate these virtues and have love and equanimity for all beings.

Buddha also did not encourage metaphysical speculations. In the Majjhima Nikaya, Sutta 63, he talks to Malunkyaputta, who questions him about the world and whether it is finite, eternal or something else. This has always been a central concern in metaphysics: is the world outside eternal or does it eventually dissolve or disappear? Is it finite or not? Buddha refuses to answer him directly. He simply says that if a man is struck by a poisoned arrow and might die, what would he tell the surgeon who came to treat him? Would he ask who shot the arrow, whether he was short or tall, what his complexion was, what his caste was and so on? Would he insist on answers before he allowed the arrows to be removed? If he insisted, he would die. In the same way, for those seeking enlightenment and a way out of suffering, it is important to follow the teachings and not waste time on such speculations. Buddha was teaching that all metaphysical speculations about the world, enlightenment and God were not important. They created only endless discussion and argumentation, doubt and loss of time and energy. Through enlightenment, all such questions would either be answered or understood as irrelevant.

Teachings for Laypersons

One set of teachings are for monks, nuns and those who aspire to Nirvana. However, Buddha has also given teachings for laypersons. These constituted the majority of his followers. On various occasions, householders approached him and asked him to teach them.

He said that a householder can also enjoy happiness. By working hard and virtuously, they can earn wealth. This gives the first kind of happiness or satisfaction of having accomplished something. The wealth itself gives enjoyment, the opportunity to share it with their family and others and also to do good deeds. Wealth also frees them from debt, which also brings happiness. Finally, if they are moral and upright, they enjoy that happiness due to blamelessness. He says the happiness of being blameless exceeds the other three kinds of happiness. He also says that after all this, the householder should examine all their actions and gain wisdom.

He even tells the monks about the benefits from virtuous householders. Such householders help others with faith, and when they die they are reborn in a good environment. Such a virtuous householder becomes like a banyan tree and provides shelter to monks as well as lay followers.

Such laypersons, irrespective of their caste or vocation, honour and respect their parents, who in turn bless them. As a result, they progress further. They also respect their spouses, children and those who work with them. They in turn wish them well and so they progress further. They respect their neighbours, who, in turn, wish them well. They also honour the deities, who in turn bless them. Finally, they respect and honour ascetics and brahmins (here, the word brahmin probably means learned person). They in turn bless them.

Such a virtuous person does his duty towards his parents, wife and children. He looks after all those who are dependent on him. He acts for the good of those relatives who are alive and even those have passed away. He helps ascetics, brahmins and the deities. He becomes worthy of veneration and praise. Such a person rejoices in heaven after death.

Another person approaches Buddha and frankly says that he wants to remain a householder, but asks for his teachings. The questioner refers to what is prohibited for monks—sense pleasures, use of sandalwood, garlands, scents, ointments and owning gold and silver—and says he enjoys them all and does not want to give them up. Buddha teaches him as follows. He tells him of those things that lead to happiness in the present and future lives. Accomplishing what one sets out to do, protecting what he has accomplished, good friends and balanced living lead to happiness.

He says that the first accomplishment is to earn a living skilfully and diligently, using sound judgement. Buddha names farming, raising cattle, archery, government service and the crafts. But we can take it to mean any means of earning a living. This leads to the happiness of accomplishment. Such a person then protects his wealth from 'kings and thieves', from the elements (fire and floods) and from unhappy heirs and relatives. This gives him the happiness of security. He is friendly with other accomplished neighbours and their families. He emulates their virtues like generosity and wisdom. This gives him the happiness from friendship. Finally he keeps track of his wealth and neither spends too little nor too much. He is not extravagant or frugal. He warns against infidelity, drunkenness, gambling and bad company, which can erode wealth.

Buddha also says that faith, virtuous behaviour, generosity and wisdom lead to happiness for the householder. He says virtuous behaviour means that one should avoid taking others' lives, stealing, sexual misconduct, falsehood, liquor, intoxicants and carelessness. Generosity means taking delight in helping others and charity. Wisdom means knowing what leads to happiness and the removal of all suffering. All this leads to the householder's welfare in this life and in future lives.

Buddha warns householders who lead an immoral or unethical life. They will lose wealth, get an evil reputation, be troubled in their mind and after death, be reborn into misery. However, those who practice virtue will gain wealth, a good reputation, be confident of themselves, have a serene death and be reborn in a happy state.

Buddha also names several householders who had either gained Nirvana or had made tremendous progress and would gain it in the very next life. He also says that 500 such persons were eventually bound for enlightenment. He is not saying that only monks gain enlightenment. But he does say that these householders had freed themselves from desires and cravings.

He also accepts the invitation of Amrapali, a courtesan. He goes there with the monks. It shows his broad-mindedness. Towards the end, he eats a meal from the hands of Cunda, and soon after, falls ill. He instructs Ananda, one his chief disciples, to tell Cunda not to feel guilty that his meal was the cause of his illness and passing away.

Buddha's teachings to monks and householders are different. He knew that the monks were striving for Nirvana. He also knew that householders wanted to lead a happy life in the world and were not interested in complete renunciation.

Buddhism and Metaphysics

We discuss this issue from the commonly accepted way of thinking about God as a creator and law-giver, different from living beings and the material universe. Buddhism is silent about it. In the Brahmajala Sutta of the Digha Nikaya of the Sutta Pitaka, Buddha refers to Brahma as creator, the Supreme Being. He also refers to various deities or minor gods. But he does not give any importance to this. His teaching is always about how to be happy here and now, how to gain Nirvana. Disputes about God are not important for him.

In the Majjhima Nikaya Sutta 72 of the Sutta Pitaka, Buddha is questioned about whether the universe is eternal and infinite. He refuses to give an answer. He is asked whether the soul and the body are the same. He again refuses to answer. He is asked whether Buddha exists after his body passes away or not. Again he refuses to answer. The questioner then asks him why he does not answer. Buddha answers, saying that holding on to views about these issues lead to distress and anguish. They do not lead to peace, insight or awakening. He is then asked whether the monk who is free is reborn or not. He asks the questioner, in turn, what remains when fire is extinguished. Where does it go? The questioner says it is not possible to say where it has gone, one can only say that the fuel has been consumed and the fire is extinguished. Buddha says that in the same way, we cannot say what happens to one who is free, whose desires have been extinguished.

In the Samyutta Nikaya of the Sutta Pitaka verse 44.10, someone asks Buddha whether there is a self or soul. He remains silent. He is then asked whether there is no self. He again remains silent. When the questioner goes away, Ananda, his chief disciple, asks him why he did not answer. Buddha says that any answer he gave him would have confused him.

Sects in Buddhism

Buddhism split into three major sects. Each of them has a large number of texts and commentaries. Here, we have focused almost entirely on the words of Buddha as found in the Sutta Pitaka. The Vinaya Pitaka has rules for monks. The Abhidhamma Pitaka was written in the third Buddhist Council, most likely during the reign of Asoka, centuries after the passing away of Buddha. These three form the basic texts of Theravada Buddhism. Abhidhamma means the higher teaching. It has very detailed discussions on human psychology and physiology and how this understanding can be applied by one who strives for Nirvana. Theravada has come to mean 'teaching of the elders'. It is in Pali and is prevalent in Sri Lanka, Myanmar, Thailand, Cambodia and Laos.

Mahayana Buddhism has its own sacred texts, which are in Sanskrit, Chinese and Tibetan. Mahayana means the great vessel, which can carry the individual to Nirvana. They are classified as Sutras, Sastras and Tantras. There are many Sutras that were written over the centuries. The earliest was perhaps the Salistamba Sutra, or the 'rice stalk sutra', and it has many things in common with the Tripitaka texts of Theravada Buddhism. The Mahayana Sutras are considered the words of Buddha, but other sects do not agree with it. It is difficult to trace the origin of many of the texts. One of the distinguishing features of

Mahayana is the development of the bodhisattva ideal. The bodhisattva strives over several lifetimes to become a Buddha, not for their own emancipation, but for the good of all beings. Mahayana is prevalent in China, Japan, Korea, Mongolia and Tibet.

A third early sect was Vajrayana Buddhism. It developed tantric practices, including repetition and chanting of mantras. It is prevalent in Tibet and Mongolia.

Some major philosophies came from Buddhism. However, all the sects of Buddhism accept that Buddha is the supreme teacher, and that the goal is Nirvana. They all accept the need for leading a moral or ethical life according to dhamma, for controlling the mind and giving up all attachments as pre-conditions for attaining Nirvana.

Buddhist *stupas*, or monuments with sacred relics of Buddha or of other saints, and temples and pagodas came up over the centuries. The temples follow rituals. They vary according to the region. They primarily worship Buddha.

Two of the national symbols in modern India are based on Buddhism. One is the emblem of the four lions found in Sarnath, where Buddha first preached the Four Noble Truths. This was erected by the emperor Asoka. This is found on all currency notes and coins and is used as a national symbol in various government offices. The second symbol is the Asoka chakra or wheel found in the middle of the Indian flag. This symbolizes the wheel of dharma from Buddhism and was first widely used by Asoka in the various monuments he built.

Notes

Among the world's great religions, Buddhism stands out because it does not talk of God or devotion to God.[*] Buddha is silent about God. The teachings are practical and easy to understand. We do not find elaborate rituals in the teachings. There were no Buddhist temples in Buddha's lifetime. Buddha's utterances give glimpses of his revelations, especially in the Udana. But they are almost devoid of metaphysics. The teachings are logical and a step-by-step guide for those who want to attain Nirvana. Buddha, however, also has teachings for laypersons on how to lead a happy life in the world. There is no distinction of caste, gender or status, either in his life or in his teachings.

The first organized monastic order was established by Buddha. Before that, there were monks who lived for a time with their teachers but they were scattered. He also allowed women to become nuns or *bhikkunis*. The first to join were his former wife and his foster mother. Later, other women also became nuns. Given the social conditions in those days, it was probably a revolutionary step. But true to

---

[*] Jainism rejects God. It has a much smaller number of followers compared to Buddhism

the vows of monasticism, the *bhikkus* and bhikkunis lived separately.

The teachings were spread all over Asia and parts of the Middle East by Buddhist monks over the next centuries. The emperor Asoka converted to Buddhism and helped spread the religion not only all over India, but also to neighbouring countries. Buddhism spread to various countries within a few centuries, well before the advent of Christianity. It was the world's largest religion at that time. It had spread to China, East, Central and South-east Asia, to the west of India, to modern-day Pakistan and Afghanistan and even to Egypt.

Buddha did not claim to be the first or only fully enlightened being. He refers to himself as the twenty-fourth Buddha in the Buddhavamsa section of the Khuddaka Nikaya in the Sutta Pitaka. He also recounts 500 tales of his previous lives in the Jataka tales. All these stories have a moral and show Buddha in previous lives as wise and compassionate. These stories are very popular. The Dhammapada is also very popular and is part of the Khuddaka Nikaya. It has stories about various people who met Buddha. For instance, one mother comes with her dead child and asks Buddha to restore him to life. He in turn asks her to go and collect mustard seeds from those nearby households where no one has died. She did the rounds of the houses and could not find a single such house. She slowly realizes that death is inevitable and comes back. He then teaches her and sends her away fully consoled.

There are separate teachings for monks and householders. For householders, the teachings are about attaining success and happiness here and now, and not after Nirvana. However, Buddhism says that householders who follow the higher teachings can also attain Nirvana.

Two key questions, on whether the universe and the soul are eternal, are not directly answered by Buddha. The philosophical implication of the universe always existing is that it is separate from God, and is 'real' in the sense that it is permanent. In Advaita, for instance, the universe is maya or a delusion, and after full enlightenment, we understand what this is. The Atman or self is eternal in Hinduism. However, in Buddhism, especially in the later philosophies, there is no permanent entity called the soul. Jainism says there is a soul, but it can change.

In practical terms, the methods of attaining Nirvana have much in common with the other Indian religions. Following moral and ethical teachings, cultivating virtuous thoughts and actions, avoiding those that cause harm, not hankering for worldly pleasures, controlling the mind and senses, meditation and so on are common to all religions.

Attaining Nirvana is a major focus of Buddhism. This leads to bliss, cessation of all sorrow and freedom from rebirth. This is the *summum bonum*, the highest or ultimate good, for human beings. Buddhism believes in karma, rebirth and liberation. All these concepts are common to other Indian religions, though the degree of emphasis varies. Buddhism is a practical religion, and does not depend on God as a creator or a saviour.

Buddhism and Jainism explicitly negate the importance of the Vedas. They are classified as *nastika* doctrines (i.e., those that refute the Vedas) in Hindu philosophy. However, some of the Hindu Puranas name Buddha as one of the Ten Incarnations of God, even though he was silent on the question of God's existence as the creator, sustainer, dissolver and lord of the Universe.

In the land of its origin, there are few Buddhists today. But Buddha continues to be revered in India. The emperor Asoka created the wheel of dharma with twenty-four spokes. It is used in the Indian national flag. The first sermon preached by Buddha in Sarnath was commemorated by Asoka with an emblem with four lions facing the four directions. This is used on all currency notes and coins. They also have a statement from the Mundaka Upanishad, 'Satyameva Jayate': truth alone triumphs.[2]

Buddhism is the world's fourth largest religion. It was the first religion to proselytize, and Buddhist missionaries spread from China in the east to Egypt and the Roman empire. No wars were fought back then in the name of Buddhism or during its spread. Buddhism was the largest religion in the world when Christianity first arose, and remained so for some centuries till Christianity took over.

It is estimated that even in India, for many centuries, Buddhism was the largest religion. Cambodia, Thailand, Burma (Myanmar), Bhutan, Sri Lanka, Laos and Mongolia are some countries with a Buddhist majority population. In recent times, there has been a renewed interest in Buddhism in the West, because of the teachings of well-known Buddhist monks from Tibet, Vietnam, Sri Lanka and other Asian countries.

5

JAINISM

Introduction

Jainism is based on the teachings of twenty four teachers called Tirthankaras.[1] The word *tirtha* in Sanskrit means a place of pilgrimage, but here it means a path or bridge for crossing over from *samsara* or the worldly life into *moksha* or liberation. The Tirthankaras are thus the Teachers who show us the way. They are supremely enlightened, have the highest knowledge, Kevala Jnana and are omniscient. The word Jain derives from *jina*, which means conqueror or victor over worldly desires, attachments and the senses. This conquest endows liberation and omniscience.[*] They are also known as *arihant*,[†] those who, after gaining omniscience, become world teachers. The last Tirthankara

---

[*] Even in Hinduism, *sanyatendriyah*, meaning control over the senses, leads to supreme peace, (Bhagavad Gita, Chapter 4.39).

[†] Arihant or arahant is also used in Buddhism to mean a person who has reached perfect enlightenment

was Mahavira, also sometimes known as Vardhaman. Mahavira means the great hero who has conquered worldly existence.

Jainism says that religion existed eternally in the universe. The teachings were heard by the Tirthankaras, who passed them on to us. However, what is available to us has come down through Mahavira, the last Tirthankara.

We have a few details of his life. There are slight differences in the way the life of Mahavira is recorded in the two major sects of Jainism, Digambara and Svetambara. Digambara literally means sky-clad, and Svetambara means clad in white.

He was said to be born in 599 BCE and passed away at the age of seventy-two in 527 BCE. The exact dates are not known with certainty. He was born into a royal family and lived the life of a prince till the age of twenty-eight or thirty. At birth, he was named Vardhaman, or one who grows and prospers. His father, Siddhartha, was a local king in the Vaishali region in modern-day Bihar in India. His mother, Trishala, was a princess from the neighbouring Lichhavi region. His mother had fourteen divine dreams foretelling that she would have a son who would become a world teacher [2].

The Digambara sect of Jains holds that he did not marry, while the Svetambara sect says he married Yashoda as instructed by his parents and had one daughter, Priyadarshana. He was brought up in luxury but was not affected by it. He left home at the age of twenty-eight or thirty in search of enlightenment. He struggled hard for many years. He underwent severe austerities, had no possessions and used only one small piece of cloth or sometimes no clothes. According an ancient tradition, monks used a begging bowl. But Mahavira did not have even that. He fasted often. He did not eat anything that was expressly cooked for him. He allowed insects to bite him without harming them. Many people thought he was mad and insulted him. He bore all these insults patiently, without any anger. He did not have a home and lived in cremation or burial grounds. He wandered from place to place except for the four months of the rainy season. This is again a tradition in India, where monks do not travel during this season.

It is believed that the twenty-third Tirthankara, Parshvanath, who preceded Mahavira, was his guru or teacher. After twelve years of intense struggle, he attained Kevala Jnana or full enlightenment, which means omniscience. After that, for the next thirty years, he preached and attracted a large number of followers. He was respected and known by several names, including Nayaputta, Muni, Samana, Nigantha, Brahman and Bhagavan. Some Buddhist texts refer to him as Araha or worthy and Veyavi or wise.

He attained Mahanirvana, i.e., gave up his physical body in the town of Pawapuri in modern-day Bihar in India. It has become a place of pilgrimage.

The Jain tradition says that Mahavira was the twenty-fourth Tirthankara. So the texts refer to the earlier Tirthankaras. This is similar to the Torah, where Moses is a major prophet, but the earlier Abrahamic prophets are also referred to. The teachings of Mahavira were not directly recorded but were committed to memory and transmitted orally.

The Sacred Texts

The sacred texts are derived from the teachings of Mahavira. His disciples, called Ganadharas, understood and memorized his teachings.

Due to famine, a large number of people who had memorized the teachings passed away. One sect says that a few survived. It was felt that the teachings would be lost and should be put down in writing. They were written down from memory. The religion also broke into two sects, the Digambara and the Svetambara. Digambara means sky-clad, and their monks do not wear any clothes. Svetambara means those who wear white clothes. Historians estimate that this split started around the third century BCE and became more complete around the fifth century CE. According to one theory, the Digambara went to south India to escape the famine.[3] Meanwhile, the texts were written down in the north. Later, when they came to know of these texts, the Digambaras did not fully accept the authenticity of the northern texts.

Svetambara Jains have a list of thirty-two sacred texts, or according to yet another schism within them, forty-five texts. They are classified into Agama or Anga Sutras, Upanga Sutras, Chedasutras, Mulasutras and appendices. Some of them are said to contain the words of Mahavira. This is not fully accepted by the Digambara sect. For them, the Ṣhaṭkhaṅḍāgama is the oldest Digambara Jain sacred text. A venerable monk called Dhrasena recalled the vast Jain scriptures and got two of his disciples to write them down, perhaps in the first century CE. Much of this sacred text is philosophy. Kundakunda of the Digambara sect was another equally venerated teacher who wrote many sacred texts like *Niyamasara* (Essence of Restraint), the *Panchastikayasara* (Essence of the Five Existents), the *Samayasara* (The Essence of the Self) and the *Pravachanasara* (Essence of Teaching). Over the centuries, several texts and commentaries have been written by various *acharyas* or teachers.

The most sacred Svetambara texts are the twelve Angas or Agamas. They are the Acharya, Sutra, Sthananga, Samavayna, Vyakhya, Jnata, Upasaka, Antakrid, Anuttaropatti, Prajna, Chhedasutra and Mulachara Angas. Each text covers one aspect of the Jain teachings. They range from teachings and practices for monks to those for householders, elaborate theories of karma to commentaries on other Angas, the lives of the Tirthankaras and other enlightened persons to what happens to the soul after death and how karma determines its journey, the stages the soul goes through before final liberation to the characteristics of a liberated soul. It also prescribes practices and rules of conduct for monks, nuns and separately for householders. The philosophical teachings in the Svetambara Angas are in harmony with the Tattvarthasutra.

The two most sacred texts for the Digambara Jains are the Shatkhandagama, dictated by Dhrasena to his pupils, Acharya Pushpadanta and Bhutabali, and the Panchastikayasara by Kundakunda. Shatkhandagama is the sacred text of six (*shat*) parts (*khanda*). It has detailed expositions on the theory of karma. The Panchastikayasara talks of five substances or *dravyas* that make up reality, but also refers to Aloka, or that which is beyond all this. These five are living beings, insentient matter, dharma and adharma and space. In the Jain texts, dharma is the principle of motion and adharma of rest. A sixth, namely time, is also mentioned as that which remains unchanging, and in which everything changes.

Both sects accept the twenty-four Tirthankaras and that the teachings came down through Mahavira, the last Tirthankara. The essence of the doctrines is almost identical. Both accept the theory of karma, the ontology (view of reality), the epistemology (means of gaining knowledge) and attaining Nirvana through removal of all karmas. They agree on the basic tenets of karma, rebirth and death, and final liberation or moksha. They are both atheistic.

However, the sects differ on some issues regarding the qualifications for gaining moksha. Since the sacred texts in the original form were only transmitted orally, and some of them were lost, there is no common set of scriptures on which both agree, except the Tattvarthasutra, written in the second century CE or a bit later. It is entirely a philosophical text and does not talk of rituals and practices. The Digambara sect maintains that since Mahavira remained without clothes, monks should also remain like that. So they insist that in the final analysis, only those who shed all clothes can attain liberation. The Svetamabara sect says that while Mahavira did remain unclothed, today it is not practical and that we can attain liberation even while wearing clothes.

There are divisions within each of the two major sects. Within Digambara tradition, there are various sub-sects like Terapanthi, Bispanthi, Taranpanthi and so on. They differ about the mode of worship and acceptance of clothed monks, called Bhattarakas, as administrative heads of religious institutions. One sect worships minor gods and goddesses. There are some major monasteries headed by different acharyas. The Svetambara tradition also has various sub-sects. One sect called *murtipujakas* believes in idol worship. Another which does not, are called *sthanakavasis.* Their monasteries are also divided into various orders.

In society, there are no major differences between the sects. In India, intermarriage is a major indicator of kinship.

So Digambara and Svetambara sects dine with each other and intermarry. In 1974, a common text acceptable to both sects called the *Saman Suttam* was brought out. It was a major effort where scholars and monks were involved. It was ratified by the spiritual heads of both the sects.

The Main Teachings

Although there are two sects and various texts, they do not differ on the essentials. The overarching theme of all the teachings is about attaining Nirvana and total knowledge or Kevala Jnana. However, it does have separate teachings for lay followers and for those who follow a purely spiritual path, the *sadhus* (monks) and *sadhvis* (nuns).

In the spiritual path, three important principles are *samyak darsana* (complete or right view of reality), *samyak jnana* (right knowledge) and *samyak charitra* (right conduct).*

The five vows taught by Mahavira form the basis of all teachings. These are:

1. Nonviolence (Ahimsa)
2. Truthfulness (Satya)
3. Non-stealing (Asteya)
4. Celibacy (Brahmacharya)
5. Non-possession/Non-attachment (Aparigraha)

---

* *samyak* is used in both the Hindu and Buddhist scriptures. It means proper, complete, correct, right.

The final goal of Kevala Jnana, enlightenment, and moksha or liberation, is the same in Buddhism and in the Hindu texts like the Upanishads, Brahma Sutras and the Bhagavad Gita.

Given the wealth of Jain literature, we focus on the essential teachings, in particular from the Tattvarthasutra and from the Saman Suttam. The word *tattva* means essence or reality, *artha* is meaning and sutra are short aphorisms. Thus Tattvarthasutra are short aphorisms about the meaning of reality. The text itself says it is a '*mokshasastra*' or the sacred text on liberation. We supplement this text with material from the important Angas of the Svetambaras and the Digambara sacred texts of Dharasena and Kundakunda.

However, Jain texts contain extensive discussions on some basic concepts. There is a description of reality (called ontology in western philosophy). This reality is as described by the fully enlightened teachers, the Tirthankaras. A wrong understanding of this cannot lead you to Kevala Jnana.

The Tattvarthasutra begins with the three bases for knowledge as mentioned earlier. Then it gives a description of reality, how it manifests and the basis of knowledge. Here we infer that this knowledge helps us know reality. It goes on to describe how knowledge is gained and different kinds of knowledge, from lower to higher, leading up to omniscience or Kevala Jnana.

In brief, reality has several dimensions. In the Tattvarthasutra, reality consists of the soul, non-soul (matter), influx (how karma infuses the soul), bondage (due to karma), stoppage (of the influx of karma), gradual detachment and liberation. As explained a little later in the Sutra, karma is a cause of bondage, and removal of all karma leads to liberation.

Sensory and scriptural knowledge are indirect. Here, the implication is that both these are obtained by instruments (senses and the mind) that are limited. Higher types of knowledge are clairvoyance, telepathy and omniscience. These three are direct knowledge. Clairvoyance refers to knowledge about objects and events not obtained through the senses. The Sanskrit term for clairvoyance is *avadhi jnana*. Telepathy allows someone to know other people's thoughts. The highest knowledge is obtained when all knowledge-obstructing karmas are removed. The Tattvarthasutra warns us that inferior knowledge and even clairvoyance can be erroneous.

It goes on to describe what the soul is. It has five characteristics, arising from subsidence, destruction, mixed, operative and intrinsic.*

In the Jain sacred texts, reality is first described. Jainism says these are the aspects of reality or existence: soul (*jīva*),

---

* Much of the debate between the Hindu and Jain texts is based on the soul. In Hinduism, the soul is unchanging.

matter (*pudgala*), space (*ākāśa*), time (*kāla*), the principle of motion (dharma) and the principle of rest (adharma).[*] It says that all these are dravyas or substances, which are eternal.[4] The main characteristic of the soul is consciousness. It describes various categories of living beings. However, all of them have souls. The idea that there are many souls, which in essence are full of knowledge, is similar to Sankhya Yoga in Hinduism. It next describes various types of matter. Matter gives the experience of pleasure, sorrow, birth and death to the soul. The modifications and changes in matter occur in time, another aspect of reality. It says that matter can be divided into smaller and smaller parts, leading to something that can no longer be divided. This is similar to the modern idea of atoms. There is a very similar idea in the Vaiseshika philosophy of Hinduism. Space and time are insentient and non-material.

In the Hindu texts, reality is described in the Shat Darsanas or six philosophies of Nyaya, Vaiseshika, Sankhya, Yoga Sutras, Purva Mimamsa and Uttara Mimamsa or Brahma Sutras, and much later in Advaita, Visishtadvaita, Dvaita and other philosophies. These texts in Hinduism have a lower status than the Upanishads, which are considered revelations. The Tripitakas of Buddhism, by contrast, do not emphasize their theory of reality, which was developed centuries later by Nagarjuna and others.

---

[*] In Sanskrit, dharma means that which bears, holds, sustains, supports.

Ontological questions are not discussed in detail in the most sacred scriptures of the Abrahamic religions. There are statements about God as creator. From this, we infer what reality is according to the Abrahamic religions.

Jain metaphysics is based on the well-known idea of *anekantavada*. It is derived from the Sanskrit words *aneka, anta* and *vada*. Aneka means many, anta here means ends and vada means philosophy. Thus, anekantavada means the philosophy of many-sided reality. Only the Kevala Jnanis or Arihants (the Tirthankaras are a special class of those with complete knowledge who become world teachers; the Arihants may not become world teachers) can have complete knowledge. For others, the doctrine of anekantavada applies. The instruments of knowledge, like the senses, mind and reason, are limited. Through them, we can get only partial knowledge. This leads to different views of reality. No matter what we say about reality, it is limited, and many views are possible.

The Jain texts also have an elaborate epistemology, i.e., the way of acquiring knowledge. After telling us what reality is, they go into the question of how to know it, the obstacles on the way, how they can be overcome and so on. Perhaps this is a unique aspect of the sacred texts. Buddhism also has detailed discussions about how to acquire knowledge.

Karma is of central importance in Jain philosophy. Karma is the cause of bondage and repeated birth and death. It obscures true knowledge, which would free us and grant us Nirvana. Jain philosophy discusses karma, what it is, how it arises, how it binds the individual and, of course, how we can be freed of it. Action of the body, mind and speech leads to influx of karma. Good actions lead to merit or *punya*, and bad ones lead to *paapa* or demerit due to sin. Passions lead to action, which gives rise to karma, which causes rebirth. The influx of karma varies and depends on the intensity of action, the motivation and the very nature of the action. Actions based on negative emotions, like jealousy and selfishness, lead to karmas that obscure knowledge. Sorrow and suffering lead to an influx of karmas that are unpleasant. Actions based on compassion lead to karmas that cause pleasant feelings. Doubts about the knowledge in the scriptures or what the knowers of truth have said leads to karmas that delude the soul. Actions based on passions lead to karmas that harm the character and cause delusion. Actions that inflict pain and sorrow lead to rebirth in hell-like regions. The consequences of deceit include rebirth as an animal or a vegetable. Mild transgressions lead to human birth. Good actions done with detachment, good intentions and having the right beliefs lead to rebirth in celestial regions. Crooked activities lead to rebirth in deformed bodies. Straightforward and honest activities are good.

It also tells us how to overcome karma. It should be noted that merely doing good activities to gain merit will not lead to Nirvana. One has to go beyond all karma. Some austerities are prescribed for this. Faith, reverence, fulfilling the vows (including the five vows mentioned earlier), pursuit of knowledge, giving gifts (*daana* or charity), practising the teachings of the Tirthankaras and compassion for all help in removing the karmas.

There are direct and simple teachings for fulfilling the five vows. The scriptures give us practices that help us fulfil each vow. For instance, Ahimsa, the first vow, can be fulfilled if we control speech, thought, food and drink, and are aware of our actions. The vow of adhering to Satya or Truth can be fulfilled by giving up anger, greed and cowardice or fear. Anger and greed can make us do wrong and deviate from truth. Fear often makes us give up truth. The vow of Asteya or non-stealing or not coveting material things can be fulfilled by residing in solitary places, not causing any problem for others, eating through *bhiksha* or alms what is prescribed and not quarrelling with others. The vow of Brahmacharya or celibacy can be fulfilled by not exposing one's senses to stories or sights that excite lust, by avoiding food that stimulates desire and by not adorning the body. The fifth vow of Aparigraha or detachment can be fulfilled by giving up attraction and aversion to enjoyment obtained through the contact of the five senses with the external world.

The scriptures provide more details about the consequences of not fulfilling the five vows. It leads to suffering, increase of bad karma and rebirth in inferior bodies below the human level if the transgressions are extreme. On the other hand, positive actions and motivations are helpful. Benevolence and compassion for all living beings, joy in the company of the virtuous, sympathy for those who suffer and tolerance towards those who insult you or behave badly also help in gaining true detachment.* Another way of gaining detachment is by seriously contemplating and understanding the nature of the world. Do we gain permanent happiness from it? Detachment develops through this process.

Or the nature of mundane existence (the universe) and the body (may also be contemplated) in order to cultivate awe at the misery of worldly existence and detachment to worldly things.

The two principal means of gaining Nirvana are mentioned: total detachment (from all worldly things) and complete concentration of mind. This automatically leads to Kevala Jnana or complete knowledge and enlightenment. However, the process to be followed is also given.

For householders who are not interested in a totally spiritual life, twelve *anuvratas* (*anu,* small, and *vrata*, vow) or minor vows are prescribed. The first five are the same as

---

* True detachment is from the body, mind and ego. It is not detachment from feelings of compassion and empathy for those who suffer—in fact this is encouraged.

the five *mahavratas* or great vows of the monks mentioned earlier. However, these vows are followed in moderation. For instance, physical relations with anyone other than one's wife is forbidden. Even in this, moderation is prescribed. The next set of three minor vows is for external activities. It includes avoiding too many activities, limited consumption and avoiding purposeless activities that may lead to sin. The final four minor vows are for inner discipline. These include regular meditation, further limiting one's activities (for instance, avoiding work and business that may lead to violence or falsehood), living for a brief period of a day or more as a monk observing all the five mahavratas and giving in charity.

The twelve minor vows make life more peaceful, reduce the accumulation of karmas, especially bad karmas, and prepare the individual for the spiritual life. They limit the accumulation of wealth and enjoyments.

The Tattvarthasutra also says that karma is a substance, *pudgala*. It describes various types of karma caused by different actions. It refers, for instance, to twenty-eight types of karmas that lead to delusion. The karmas come to fruition at some time or the other, and the individual has to experience the consequences. These have to be borne with fortitude, taking care not to add further binding karmas by reacting in the wrong way. Even the saints and the Tirthankaras are subject to karma. It describes the experiences or suffering one has to undergo due to different types of karma that have come to fruition. All the other Indian religions, namely, Hinduism, Buddhism and Sikhism also say that everyone has to experience the outcome of their karma.

Through right conduct and austerity, the karmas can be overcome. Meditation is concentration on one object. Kevala or perfect knowledge is attained by destroying all different types of karmas—those that delude (*moha*), those that cover perception and knowledge and those that obstruct. *Nirjara* is the removal of all the karmas from the soul and leads to moksha or liberation.

The Tattvarthasutra has a famous aphorism which is regarded as a motto by Jains. This is *Parasparopagraho Jivanam*. Etymologically, *paraspara* means mutual, and *upagraha* here means support. Jivanam means all living beings. The aphorism says that all living beings support each other. By common interpretation, this means not only helping each other as human beings, but also helping animals and not harming or being violent towards any living being. This is a key aspect of Jainism in everyday life.

Some Important Teachings of Mahavira

He taught the five great vows to monks: Ahimsa or non-violence, Satya or truth, Asteya or non-stealing, Brahmacharya or celibacy and Aparigraha or non-accumulation of wealth. Some of his well-known teachings are given below.

'There are no external enemies. The real enemies are internal and include anger, pride, greed, attachment and hate.'

'There is no use fighting with external enemies. Fight with yourself. He who conquers himself gets great happiness.'

'It is better to conquer one's own self than to overcome countless enemies.'

'The soul comes alone and goes alone. No other soul accompanies it when the body dies.'

'If you cannot withstand pain on your own body and mind, what right do you have to inflict it on others?'

The gist of the teachings are non-violence, self-restraint and following spiritual disciplines. This is the principal method of overcoming karma and hence gaining liberation. There are separate teachings for laypersons who have not renounced worldly life. But the moral and ethical teachings are very similar, though the vows are not so strict.

Jain Mythology

Like all religions, Jainism also has texts with mythology. In the life of Mahavira itself, his mother has fourteen auspicious dreams foretelling the birth of a great soul. Mahavira also had ten dreams indicating that he would be fully enlightened in the near future. All these dreams were symbolic and were interpreted to understand what they meant. There were dreams about an elephant, a bull, a lion, a milky white sea, smokeless fire and so on. The lion is taken to be a symbol of strength and power and is shown in many of the seated sculptures of Mahavira on the plinth below his legs. Mahavira, literally the great hero, conquered himself and is more powerful than a lion.

The Kalpa Sutra, one of the twelve Angas or Agamas of the Svetambara tradition, has the stories of the twenty-four Tirthankaras. For instance, the first Tirthankara, Rishabh Deva or Adinath, had twelve births before his final birth as a Tirthankara. Some of these lives were as a celestial being in heaven. After each human birth, he gained enough merit to be born as a celestial being. In his last human birth as a Tirthankara, his mother has fourteen dreams foretelling the birth of a great soul. On his birth, the gods in heaven rejoiced and took him briefly for a celestial ceremony. He later got married to two women, through whom he has more than a hundred children. However, one day, he developed strong detachment and renounced his kingdom and family. He went away in search of enlightenment. After a long struggle, he came a Tirthankara. According to some legends, he was very tall—some say over a thousand feet—and lived for thousands of years. Similar mythological stories are told about all the Tirthankaras.

Mallinath, the nineteenth Tirthankara, was female, according to the Svetambara tradition. She took only three births to become a Tirthankara. However, the Digambara tradition does not agree that a female can be a Tirthankara.

Mahavira was the last Tirthankara. His twenty-seven previous births are recorded. He was first born as a woodcutter. He was later born as the grandson of the first Tirthankara, Rishabh Deva. During the twenty-seven births, he was also occasionally born as a celestial being. He was also born in the lowest, seventh hell after one life where he committed violent sins. This was the cause of Mahavira's great suffering in his final birth. Even the Tirthankaras cannot escape the consequences of karma. He had to be born as a lion. He bore this life with fortitude. As a result, he was born as a human in his next life. In his twenty-fifth birth, he performed severe austerities. As a result, he was born as a celestial being. In his final, twenty-seventh birth, he was born as a Tirthankara—as predicted by the first Tirthankara, Rishabh Deva, whose grandson he was earlier.

Mythology is part of every religion. Even Jainism and Buddhism, which are based on reason and logic, have mythology. These were written centuries after the religion was first established. It is said that in the case of Jainism, Bhadrabahu is credited with the authorship of the Kalpa Sutras in the fourth century BCE, about a hundred years after the passing away of Mahavira. However, it was put down in writing several centuries later. Buddhism also has a rich mythology, including the Jataka tales recounting the previous lives of the Buddha. Hinduism has even more extensive mythological stories in the Puranas, and perhaps interpolated in the Ramayana and the Mahabharata, which probably predated Jainism and Buddhism.

These mythological stories probably reached a far larger number of people back then, who were not educated. The intellectually rigorous philosophies of Jainism may not have interested such a large number of people.

Jain Philosophy

Jain philosophy is focused on attaining Nirvana, freedom from the cycle of birth and death. Karma is the basis for being in bondage. Removing all karmas leads to moksha as well as complete enlightenment or Kevala Jnana.

It is based on the *ratnatraya* or three jewels: right belief, right knowledge and right conduct. They emphasize that right understanding is the first step on the path to liberation. All the important texts of both sects talk of the five or six substances that constitute reality—souls, matter, motion, rest, space and time. It goes on to say that they are eternally real. This implies that there is no creator as creation of anything would imply that it is not eternal. The world also operates according to the law of karma and other laws, which are also always operating.

So there is no need for a creator who governs the universe. In this sense, the twin roles of God as creator and ruler or governor of the universe are not required. Jainism is explicitly atheistic. This is in contrast to all other religions of the world. Buddhism does not either affirm or negate God. Some of the Hindu philosophies also are either silent about God or seem to negate the need for God. Some Hindu philosophies like Nyaya, Vaiseshika and Sankhya say the world always exists, and by implication, there is no need of God.

The Jain concept of the soul is also unique. In Jainism, the soul is eternal but changing. Karma clings to it. The soul evolves over several lives and eventually becomes free. Buddhism, with its own unique concepts, holds that there is no reality called the soul. Hinduism says that the soul is eternal, of the nature of consciousness and unchanging.

The philosophy distinguishes between the Kevala Jnana of the fully enlightened person and the knowledge of others. For an ordinary person, the philosophy of anekantavada applies. The well-known parable of the five blind men and the elephant is given. Each man touches a different part of the elephant and says it is a rope, a pillar, a wall and so on. They have only a partial understanding of reality. Similarly, anekantavada says that all beings can have only a limited or partial view of reality.

Karma is not merely activity, it is a subtle form of matter and envelops the soul. Depending on the activity and the intention, the karma that flows into the jiva can give rise to various fruits like happiness, sorrow, delusion and so on. Activity and intention also determine how thickly karma envelops the soul.

Jain philosophy is subtle and nuanced. It goes into great detail about the nature of reality. For instance, there are six substances or dravyas that constitute reality, as mentioned earlier. These undergo change and modifications, but do not change in essence. They refer to the soul, matter, space, motion and rest as the five substances that constitute reality. This is in contrast to some of the Hindu philosophies, which say that anything that is born, and therefore dies and thus changes, is not real in the final analysis. The soul is eternal and does not change even when it apparently goes from one body to another. However, Jain philosophy says the soul is eternal but undergoes changes. Perhaps the issue is how the word 'jiva' is translated. In Hindu texts, jiva is the individual, while in Jain texts it is the Atman or soul. In Jainism, the jiva in its purest form is the same as the Hindu Atman—conscious or aware and full of bliss.

There are many souls and each is different from the other, except in its purest form. This is again different from Hinduism. Even Sankhya in Hinduism, which accepts that there are many souls, says they are all identical and unchangeable.

The philosophical texts go deep into the nature of reality. For instance, in Panchastikayasara (the essence of the five existences), the author Kundakunda goes into what a substance is and its qualities. Are they separate from each other or not? If substance is separate, then it can change into many other substances. If the qualities are separate, then there is no need for the substance. It says that we cannot say the following things: that substance and qualities are identical, that they are entirely separate or that they are both distinct and identical. It argues that substance and quality imply both aspects of distinctness and separateness. Similarly, the soul and knowledge cannot be said to be entirely separate.

Jain philosophy has another distinct feature, namely dharma and adharma, which are two of substances of reality. These two words are understood differently in Jainism and in Hinduism. In Hinduism, the etymological meaning of dharma is 'that which holds, supports and sustains' the universe. In Jainism, dharma is usually translated as the medium that supports motion. The Panchastikayasara gives the powerful analogy of water in which fish move to illustrate what dharma means. If we say that the world is always changing, and so in motion, then dharma is that which supports everything. In this interpretation, there is no difference between Jainism and Hinduism—the water is the medium that supports the movement of fish (Jainism), or it is the medium that holds, supports and sustains fish (Hinduism).

Adharma in Hinduism means going against dharma. Clearly, this is not the sense in which adharma is used in

Jain philosophy. It means that which gives rest. Anything in motion can also be at rest. Without the principle of rest, anything in motion would never stop. In Jainism, adharma is the principle of rest or that which puts limits on motion. Since Jainism does not accept God, and accepts the reality of the world, the three obvious aspects—sentient beings, insentient matter and space—are not enough to describe the world. There is a dharma or law according to which living beings and matter function (or move) in space. There is a principle that puts limits on this function or movement, and that is adharma. For theistic religions, dharma and adharma are perhaps taken care of by God who is the Lord of the universe He (or She) created. Jainism's contribution to philosophy is an explanation of reality without referring to God.

In terms of practices and methods for gaining Nirvana, there is much in common with other Indian religions. The need to remove the effects of karma, austerity, cultivating positive emotions, avoiding negative emotions, meditation, faith and so on are common to all Indian religions. In fact, some of these are common to all the world's religions.

Some of the unique contributions of Jain philosophy are:

1. Emphasis on Ahimsa or non-violence. While all other religions also mention it, only Jainism makes it a central part of its teaching.

2. It is the only religion that explicitly negates the need of God as creator and sustainer of the universe.

3. It has a logical and well-developed ontology or concept of reality, and epistemology or means of gaining that knowledge. The description of reality with its five substances (six if we include time) is unique among world religions, though Nyaya, Vaiseshika and Sankhya philosophies in Hinduism also give different explanations of reality without the aid of God.

A Brief History of Jainism

There were other religions and sects at the time of Mahavira, who was senior to Buddha in age and lived and preached in the same large region in northern India in the modern regions of Bihar and Uttar Pradesh (the Digambara Jains say that as a Tirthankara, Mahavira did not travel and preach, while the Svetambaras say he did). Buddhism, with its middle path avoiding too much austerity, and its proselytizing nature, was growing. Other materialist philosophies like Charvaka or Lokayata were also there, appealing to those who did not want to struggle. Historians estimate that there were more than sixty competing philosophies at that time.

With its emphasis on non-violence, strict austerity and not making any effort to convert people, Jainism did not grow at the same rate. Dedicated Ganadharas or those who had understood, memorized and practiced the teachings kept the religion alive. According to the Svetamabra tradition, Chandragupta Maurya, one of the earliest kings of the Magadha empire, was converted to Jainism by Bhadrabahu, a great Jain teacher, in the fourth century BCE, about a hundred years after the Mahanirvana of Mahavira.

To avoid recurring famine, Bhadrabahu went to Karnataka in south India with his disciples and followers. Apparently, Chandragupta Maurya also went with him, although all the historical texts do not agree on this. Meanwhile, back in the north, Sthulabhadra asked his followers to put down in writing the sacred texts, which so far had largely remained oral. When Bhadrabahu returned, he was disappointed with the texts, which he felt were made less austere due to the famine prevailing there. Back in the south, dedicated Jain monks converted some of the Hindu kings to Jainism.

Jainism spread to some coastal regions of Andhra Pradesh and Odisha. The Svetambara texts were said to have been accepted as final in Vallabhi in Gujarat in the fifth century CE. The Digambara texts were composed starting in the first century CE.

Many of the sacred texts, particularly of the Digambara Jains, remained in the custody of monasteries and were not available to the public. Extensive commentaries totalling over 1,00,000 verses were written on just two of the Digamabara texts, the Shatkhandagama and the Kashyaprabhrita.

By the middle ages, Jainism became concentrated in some regions. The western region of Rajasthan and Gujarat has a greater concentration compared to the south-central region of Maharashtra, Madhya Pradesh and Karnataka.

Jain Practices and Rituals

Here, we focus on rituals and practices for laypersons. There are numerous Jain temples in India for both the Digambara and Svetambara sects. They usually have idols of the Tirthankaras. They are not regarded as gods but are highly revered. Some rituals are followed in the temples. These include lighting of lamps, bowing to the images and recitation from the holy texts. There is a priest who conducts all the rituals. The Tirthankaras cannot directly help since they have gained moksha and freedom from rebirth. However, it puts the mind of the person offering reverence into a proper frame for meditation.

Jains believe that austerity, charity and alms giving helps not only in the spiritual life, but also leads to material gain. Many Jains are highly successful in business and have accumulated wealth. This is in contrast to the austere life of the monks and nuns. However, the wealth enables them to support the monastic communities, the temples and also give in charity.

Daily rituals are prescribed for Jain householders. It includes bathing and worship. Some meditation is also prescribed. There are periodic fasts, which remove karmas. Ritual fasting at two different times of the year is part of the austerities called Paryushan by the Svetambaras and Das Lakshana Dharma by the Digambaras. It lasts from eight to ten days and requires complete fasting, with only boiled water drunk between sunrise and sunset. Meditation and seeking forgiveness are part of the austerities.

There are very few practical teachings about meditation except to say that it is based on concentration. Presumably, these methods are passed on from teacher to disciple over the ages.

Notes

Jainism evolved after Mahavira. But some aspects of its philosophy were present in earlier texts. Jainism itself says their religion is eternal. In Buddhism, there is a record of Buddha telling his disciples to go and spread the dhamma or teaching. In Jainism, there is no such teaching from Mahavira. It is therefore a non-proselytizing religion. This also true of Judaism, Hinduism and Sikhism. The number of people adhering to these religions has never seen rapid growth at any point in history, unlike Buddhism, Christianity and Islam, which are proselytizing religions.

Even within the land of its birth, Jainism moved away from the Bihar regions and took root in western India and parts of southern India. The reasons for this are not known. Perhaps it has to do with famines that were recorded at that time in the region of its origin. Jains may have migrated away from there.

It remains the smallest religion in India. Though estimates vary, it is very likely that there are less than 5 million followers or less than 0.4 per cent of the population. Most of the followers are in India, though there are small numbers who live in other countries, including in the West. Jainism does not accept the caste system. However, some traditional marriages arranged by family elders between Jains and Hindus take place. It is usually between Jains and people from the business or merchant castes in Hinduism.[5]

In India, Jains live in harmony with other religions. Jains also celebrate India's most famous festival, Deepavali or Diwali, known as the festival of lights. For Jains, the day coincides with the day of enlightenment and final Nirvana of Mahavira. Many Hindus are only vaguely aware that Jains are a different religion or what its central tenets are. They are only aware that Jains are vegetarians.

The emphasis on vegetarianism, prohibition of all vegetables that grow underground, taking care not to harm or kill any insects even if they are troublesome, a greater focus on austerity and negation of God and the Vedas are special features of Jainism. Jain monks traditionally do not shave their head but pluck their hairs out. Digambara monks do not wear any clothes and remain naked. The monks' daily life and activities are also restricted and austere. Perhaps very few were attracted towards Jain monasticism. Lay followers in ancient times accepted a new religion based on the life and teachings of the monks because they did not read the sacred texts. While people admired the religion, they were not willing to follow all its principles and practices.

Buddhism, by contrast, was a proselytizing religion and did not advocate severe austerity. It got a boost when the emperor Asoka embraced Buddhism. In any case, whatever the reason may have been, Jainism did not grow. At the same time, Jainism has survived since the days of Mahavira. Buddhism, which at one point was a dominant religion in India, hardly has any followers from ancient times. Recently, many Buddhist refugees from Tibet came to India, and many followers of Dr Ambedkar converted from Hinduism to Buddhism. So the numbers have grown. But Jainism has continued unbroken in India since the sixth century BCE.

6

SIKHISM

A Short Life History of Guru Nanak

The Sikh religion was founded by Guru Nanak. He was born in 1469 CE in Talwandi, now called Nankana Sahib, close to the city of Lahore in present-day Pakistan. His parents were Kalyan Chand Das Bedi (Mehta Kalu) and Mata Tripta, who were Hindu Khatris. Nanak had a sister, Nanaki. His father was a revenue official with the local landlord of Talwandi. As a child, Nanak was was intelligent and learnt the basics of reading, writing and arithmetic from local teachers. He was said to be very generous even in childhood, giving away things in charity and spending time in meditation. He spent time with wandering sadhus in the forests. He was also taught Sanskrit and Persian. Though he learnt fast, he was not interested in mundane education. Since he was quiet and took little interest in studies, the elders in his family thought that a ghost had got hold of him and tried to get it exorcised. The exorciser understood that this was not the case and went away. Nanak was also sent to graze cattle as he showed no interest in his studies.

His family wanted to conduct his *upanayana*, the thread ceremony, in which high-caste boys are given a sacred mantra and a thread to wear around their chest. However, the young Nanak said he wanted the thread of compassion, contentment and continence that would never break. During such incidents, he composed some highly spiritual *shabads* (from the Sanskrit *shabda*, meaning word) or verses, even at that age. It is said that these were later introduced in the Guru Granth Sahib, the sacred text of Sikhism.

He was married at sixteen to Sulakhani. He continued his quiet life, did not do any work to earn money and spent time in meditation. His father got more worried. In one incident, the young Nanak was given some money to start a business that would earn profits. He went and used it to feed wandering holy men and said that this was more profitable than any business. Thus another four years passed.

When Nanak was around twenty years old, his brother-in-law Jairam had an important job with the local chieftain in the town of Sultanpur. He asked Nanak's father to send him there so that he could get him a job. Nanak agreed and worked in the store of the chieftain. People used to draw rations in lieu of salary from the *modikhana* or store.

He was very honest and good in his work, and helpful to the poor. He did not indulge in the prevailing practice of keeping a tenth of the rations for himself. He became well-known and was highly respected for his honesty. He even gave away rations from his own share to holy men. Nanak brought his wife over to Sultanpur. At this time, he had two sons, Sri Chand and Lakhmi Das.

Hearing of his good work, his childhood friend Mardana came from Talwandi to see him. Though he was a Muslim, Nanak had him stay in his house. Mardana observed that Nanak used to get up early, go to the river for a bath and spend time in meditation. They had earlier planned to go on a pilgrimage but had postponed the idea as Mardana's daughter had to be married. Mardana now requested Nanak's financial help in getting this done. Nanak had become highly respected and some rich people came forward to help. Mardana was able to get his daughter married. He then came back to Sultanpur to be with Nanak.

Nanak would feed the poor and wandering ascetics. His father and mother-in-law were worried and came to Sultanpur. They told his sister Nanaki that with a family to support, he should not fritter away their wealth like this. However, Nanaki said that they had enough for everyone.

At this time, tradition says that Nanak one day did not come out of the river when he went to bathe. People thought he had drowned and tried their best to find his body. Meanwhile, Nanak had a vision where God instructed him to lead a holy life, repeat God's name, do good to the poor, remain unattached in the world and spread God's message among the people. At this time, Nanak also composed a shabad in God's praise. It is said that the *mool mantar* (the foundation mantra) of the Guru Granth Sahib was composed at this time.

Nanak emerged from the river charged with a divine mission. He was found three days later meditating in a cremation ground. The first words he uttered were 'there is no Hindu, there is no Muslim', meaning there is only one God who is not separate for different religions. He gave away all his possessions and started living with ascetics or fakirs. His wife went to live with her parents along with her younger son. The elder son remained with his aunt Nanaki. The Muslim chieftain was forced to call Nanak to answer charges of blasphemy. He first refused to go when told that some ruler was calling him. When called a second time in the name of God, he went. The Muslim cleric or *qazi* asked him how he could say there was no Muslim, and did not the Prophet Mohammad preach a true religion? Nanak replied that a true Muslim had to have faith in God, make himself pure and surrender his ego to God. The qazi asked him whether he was a Hindu or a Muslim. Nanak replied that he was on the path to God, and God was neither a Muslim nor a Hindu. He was asked to accompany them to the mosque for prayers, which he did. People were alarmed and thought he would convert to Islam. But his sister Nanaki had full faith in her brother's wisdom.

Nanak had cut off all worldly ties and along with Mardana, prepared himself for his mission. He spent more time in meditation and lived for some days on milk. They started travelling on foot to spread the message of God. It is said that they undertook four pilgrimages of several years each. In the first one, they went from Punjab towards Delhi. They met various types of people, ascetics, Muslims, those from different sects and others. The dialogues with them are recorded. Nanak sometimes pointed out the hypocrisy of prevailing religion, where ritual dominated true spiritual seeking. The recurrent message is to repeat the divine name, which leads one to God. He and Mardana went to Panipat, Hardwar, Kurukshetra, Delhi, Ayodhya, Varanasi, Prayag, Gaya, Bodh Gaya, Patna, Bengal, what is now Bangladesh and Assam. In Delhi, he is said to have met the emperor of the Lodi dynasty. It is also believed that he met Kabir, the famous saint of Varanasi, and the great saint Chaitanya at Jagannath Puri.

From here, he moved south. He went to Ganjam, Guntur and then to Kanchipuram, which is close to modern-day Chennai. He went to the pilgrimage centre of Siva, in Tiruvannamalai, and then to the Vishnu pilgrimage centre of Srirangam, which has a large temple complex. It is said that he even went to Sri Lanka. He returned via Rameswaram, Bidar, Bharuch, Girnar, Ujjain, Rajasthan,

Mathura, Delhi and to Talwandi. They had returned after twelve years. Mardana visited his home, but Nanak did not. It is said that his parents came to meet him.

He is said to have made another long journey with Mardana by foot through the Himalayas towards northeast India. His final journey was to Mecca. He met several Muslim saints and scholars. By this time, Guru Nanak had gained more experience through his travels than almost any other saint before him. His conversations with Hindus, Muslims, saints and spiritual seekers of various denominations from all over India and even as far as Mecca are unique. Apart from his message of the divine name, service to all and giving up the ego, what also stands out is his acceptance of people of all types, castes, religions and languages.

He is said to have witnessed the damage caused by the invasion of Babur, who later became the first Mughal emperor in India. Babur came from Central Asia as the rulers in Delhi had become weak. Nanak advised Babur against violence and urged him to release innocent prisoners, which he apparently did.

Based on his verses composed over the years, the Japji was selected by one of his disciples and endorsed by Guru Nanak himself. It has the mool mantar and thirty-eight other *shaloks* (or verses). Jap means repetition of the divine name with devotion and concentration. Towards the end of his life, Guru Nanak chose Bhai Lehna, his closest disciple, as his successor. He named him 'Anga', meaning he was a limb or part of Guru Nanak. Though the Guru's sons were also staying with him, they were not chosen as successors.

Guru Nanak had a premonition of his end. He passed away on 22 September 1539 CE. His disciples became known as Sikhs. Perhaps it came from the Sanskrit work *shishya*, meaning disciple. Today, a Sikh is a follower of Guru Nanak and the teachings in the sacred book, the Guru Ganth Sahib.

The Sacred Text

The Guru Ganth Sahib is the sacred text of the Sikhs. It was first complied by Guru Arjan Dev in 1604 and installed in the Golden Temple in Amritsar. In 1704, Guru Gobind Singh added some verses from his father Guru Teg Bahadur to the original Adi Granth. This was compiled and was declared as the final version, called the Guru Granth Sahib. There were different versions in different gurdwaras at that time. This issue was resolved by the final version compiled under Gobind Singh's direction.

It consists of 5,894 shabads or poetic verses composed in musical from. Although all of it is not sung, the bulk of it is set to thirty-one ragas from Hindustani classical music. It is written in the Gurmukhi script, but has Punjabi, Sanskrit, various dialects of Hindi, Persian, Arabic, Sindhi and Marathi verses.

Six of the Gurus contributed to the contents of the text. The first was Guru Nanak himself, who provided 974 verses. This includes the opening mool mantar and the Japji. These are considered the most sacred.

In addition to the six Gurus, there are verses from various saints. They are categorized as *bhagats, bhatts* and *gursikhs*. Bhagats are saints from both the Hindu and Islamic traditions. Some of the famous bhagats whose verses were taken verbatim and introduced into the Guru Granth Sahib are Kabir, Ramanand, Namdev, Surdas and Jaidev. Some of them predated Guru Nanak. During his long years of travel on foot, Guru Nanak came across these verses. One Muslim saint in this list is Baba Farid, a thirteenth century Punjabi saint. He also started the *langar* (Persian word meaning place for feeding the poor). Guru Nanak liked the idea of a langar very much and introduced it in Sikhism as well. Bhatts were Brahmins who became followers of Sikhism, mostly of Guru Arjan Dev. Their verses were also included. Gursikhs were those who were especially devoted to Sikhism. Some of their verses were also included in the sacred text. The most famous was Mardana, the companion of Guru Nanak. However, some dispute that the verses were composed by Mardana.

The Guru Granth Sahib is therefore a composition of the words of various spiritual people, most of whom were saints in their own right. It is also very eclectic, containing many languages and quoting saints of different Hindu denominations and Muslims. The running theme is always God and how to seek Him. A chant or verse attributed to Guru Gobind Singh is as follows:

'Aagya Bhai Akal Ki, Tabhe Chalaya Panth, Sabh Sikhan Ko Hukam Hai, Guru Manyo Granth, Guru Granth Ji Manyo, Pargat Gurah Ki Deh, Jo Prabh Ko Millibo Chahae, Khoj Shabad Mei Lai. Raj Karega Khalsa*, Aaki Rahe Na Koe, Khwaar Hoe Sabh Milenge, Bache Sharan Jo Hoe.'

'Under orders of the Timeless One, the Panth (Sikh religion) was created. All Sikhs have to accept the Guru Granth Sahib (sacred text), which was manifest by the Guru (or God). Those who want to find God can find Him in the sacred hymns. The Pure shall rule, not anyone else. Those separated will be united, and all will be saved.'

The sacred book is kept in the centre of the gurdwara. Devotees typically prostrate before it and seek blessings.

Secondary texts are *janam sakhis*, which contain the hagiographical account of the life of Guru Nanak, and the *rahit nama* or code of conduct of the Khalsas. The Dasam Granth is a compilation of Guru Gobind Singh's writings.

---

* The word Khalsa is derived from Arabic and means pure. Khalsa also refers to Sikhs.

The Early History of Sikhism

From 1539 CE till 1708 CE, there were a succession of nine Gurus after Guru Nanak. The period was marked by an expansion in the number of followers, establishment of various gurdwaras or temples, opening of schools, compilation of the Guru Granth Sahib and establishment of the langar (common free dining) in all gurdwaras.

There was brewing conflict with the Muslim rulers of the region. It is interesting that the first Mughal emperor, Babur, invaded India at the time of Guru Nanak, and the last Mughal emperor, Aurangzeb, passed away in 1707, one year before the last Guru, Gobind Singh. Thus, the Guru period overlapped with the Mughal empire. However, Islam had been prevalent in India for some centuries before that.

The conflict could have arisen for several reasons. The influence of the Gurus increased and they had a large following. They did not bow down to any earthly emperor but only to God. The governors of Punjab felt uncomfortable with the rising power of the Sikhs. The fifth Guru, Arjan Dev, was killed on the orders of the Mughal emperor Jahangir. This led to the formation of an army of Sikh warriors by the next Guru, Har Gobind. The ninth Guru, Teg Bahadur, was beheaded on the orders of Mughal emperor Aurangzeb. His son, Guru Gobind Singh, became the next Guru.

Gobind Singh was also in conflict with the Mughal emperors. He lost all his four sons. Two were killed in battle and two young sons were murdered. He founded the Khalsa Panth. Khalsa means pure, and Panth means sect. In 1699, he called all Sikhs to come to Anandpur. He spoke to the congregation and said that he wanted one head to be sacrificed. After some silence, one person got up. He was taken into a tent and the Guru came out with his sword dripping in blood. He asked for four more people to come forward. At the end, the tent was opened to reveal that the people who came forward were unharmed, but five goats had been sacrificed.

These five were called the Panj Pyaras (the five beloved). The Guru asked them to take initiation by dipping their sword in a pot of water. He himself took initiation from the Panj Pyaras. It is interesting that these five came from five different parts of the country and from different castes. Later, some of the Panj Pyaras were killed in battle.

Gobind Singh introduced the idea of the members of the Khalsa keeping a sword and long hair. Later, other symbols like a comb, a wrist bracelet and shorts were also introduced. Their major task was to defend religion. Many people came forward and joined the Panth. Over time, all male Sikhs adopted this dress code, whether they became warriors or not.

Gobind Singh found time amid all this to study and complete the Guru Granth Sahib. He added some verses of his own, added those by his father Guru Teg Bahadur, who had been beheaded and got a new version written.

This has become the final Guru Granth Sahib. He also said that after him, there would be no more human Gurus. The sacred text itself would be the Guru. He laid the foundation for modern Sikhism. He was assassinated by some enemies from the emperor's army. All his family—his father, four sons and Gobind himself—thus became martyrs.

The Harmandir Sahib, also known as Darbar Sahib or more famously as the Golden Temple of Amritsar, is central to Sikhism today. The word Amritsar is derived from the words Amrit Sarovar, meaning lake of nectar (or immortality). The fourth Guru, Ramdas, built the city of Amritsar. He invited some well-known businessmen to come and settle there. He himself also did the same. The lake was enlarged. The next Guru, Arjan Dev, got the temple built on the lake. Construction started in 1589 and was completed in 1604. A copy of the Adi Granth compiled by Arjan Dev was installed in the temple. Unfortunately, the temple was attacked and damaged or destroyed at least three times by the Muslims. But each time, the Sikhs took back control and rebuilt the temple. Raja Ranjit Singh overlaid the dome with gold-plated copper in 1830, and hence it is known as the Golden Temple.

The Major Teachings

The Guru Granth Sahib begins with the sacred mool mantar of Guru Nanak.

'Ik o'nkār saṯ nām karṯā purakh nirbhao nirvair
akāl mūraṯ ajūnī saibha'n gur parsāḏ.
aadh sach jugaadh sach ‖
hai bhee sach naanak hosee bhee sach'

One Om, name of Truth, doer and creator, fearless, without hatred. Beyond Time, yet manifest, unborn, Self-Existent. By Guru's Grace (it can be realized). In the beginning was the truth. True age after age. True here and now. Nanak says truth is now and will always remain.

It is a meditative mantra and came out of his spiritual realization. This is followed by the Japji of thirty-eight verses. *Japa* in Sanskrit means uttering prayer in a low voice. It refers to repetition of the sacred set of syllables. If done properly, it is said to confer divine blessings and spiritual enlightenment. Guru Nanak himself refers to this several times in his later verses.

The Japji starts off by praising God, who is all-knowing and all-powerful. It then has an important phrase, '*hukmai sabko andar*', meaning the Commander (or God) is inside everyone, there is no commander out there. It says we should be humble and not consider ourselves great. Many sing His praises and describe His glory. But few follow His commands. We need to be humble and beg the Lord's mercy. He then gives in abundance (he is clearly referring to spiritual wealth). It then says that purity is important to get divine wealth. Bad deeds or karma obscures that wisdom and we need to purify ourselves from the inside. He says that love of God and japa in the early mornings makes you pure.

It continues to praise God as One who cannot be limited, as pure, with endless virtues. By prayer and humility, God can be realized. The Guru's sacred word is the Veda and protects you. Referring to the Hindu gods, it says that the Guru is Siva, Gorakh, Brahma, Parvati and Lakshmi. Those who know Him cannot describe Him. Have no doubt that all worship the same God. At the same time, the phrase 'aisa naam niranjan hoe, jay ko man jaanai man ko-ay' is repeated several times in the short Japji. The divine word, 'naam', is pure, and if the mind knows this, it knows this (truth). While praying to God, singing his glories, repeating the divine name and so on, he is telling us to recall that everything is in the mind that is purified by God's name.

He describes saints and sinners and says he cannot understand God's ways. He prays for protection. The dirty body can be bathed, soiled clothes can be washed and similarly, the impure mind can be cleaned by the divine name. Karma binds us and makes us take repeated births. He again extols humility and says that the arrogant cannot attain God. He who is blessed to sing his glory is the king of kings. The phrase 'aad aneel anaad anaahat jug jug ayko vays' is repeated four times. It describes the formless God as the primal or first, pure, without beginning, without end, that is there age after age. It ends by saying that those who have meditated on God's name are radiant and are saved.

The word 'naam' or divine name is repeated thirteen times and truth or '*sach*' fifteen times in the Japji, showing their importance. There are references to Hindu gods like Siva, Brahma, Rama, Krishna, Parvati and Lakshmi.

The rest of the Guru Granth Sahib elaborates the core teaching in the Japji. Most of it is spiritual. In one of the shabads, Guru Arjan Dev says: 'God, let me take your refuge. All doubts ceased when I got your darsan or vision. You knew my agony even without my telling you, and you made me repeat your name. Then I danced in joy, singing your praises. You took hold of my hand and led me out of the well of delusion or maya. Say that Nanak the Guru, cut all worldly bondages and made my soul one with God.' Another well-known shabad is sung and starts with 'O mind, why are you going to the forest to search? God dwells everywhere'. The way of removing bad karma is also explicitly stated:

'*Har Naam Salaahee Rang Sio Sabh Kilavikh Kirakhaa* ||' (GGS Ang 650*)

'Praise the Lord's Name with love, and eradicate all sins.'

---

* GGS – Guru Granth Sahib, Ang means page, and the GGS is divided into pages.

This is a widespread belief in Hinduism also, especially on the path of devotion or *bhakti*. Repetition of the divine name leads to liberation. In the Bhagavad Gita, Krishna says, '*Yajna naam japayagnosmi*', meaning 'among the sacrifices, I am japa'.

Nanak sings in ecstasy in Ang 732 about the joy of the divine name. One verse is:

'*Mil sangat har rang paa-i-aa jan nanak man tan rany*' (GGS Ang 732)

'In the company of devotees (sangat), love of the Lord is obtained. Nanak's mind and body are drenched with it.'

Several saints have said this. For instance, Kabir uses the phrase '*sara tan kanchan hoe*', meaning that the entire body becomes golden with the love of the Lord.

The concept of harmony of religions is seen for the first time with verses like this:

'*Kudharath Vaedh Puraan Kathaebaa Kudharath Sarab Veechaar ||*'

'By His power the Vedas and the Puranas exist, and the holy scriptures or kitab (of the Jewish, Christian and Islamic religions). By His power all views (or religions) exist.'

There are practical teachings as well. For instance, it says that if we desire our welfare, we should do virtuous deeds and be humble (GGS, Ang 465). It also tells us what virtue and vice do to us. 'O Nanak, the wrongs we do are the chains around the neck. If one has virtues, sins are cut away and virtues become one's friend' (GGS Ang 595).

The status of women is explained clearly:

'We are born of women, we are engaged and married to women. They are our friends, and the human race continues because of her. When she dies, man seeks another wife. Why then criticize her from whom the great are born, and women are born? Nanak says, only the Lord is not born from her' (GGS Ang 473).

Practical effort is also extolled. *'Aapan hathhee apanaa aapae hee kaaj savaareeai'* means with our own hands, let us work and resolve our affairs (GGS Ang 474).

The Sikh religion is based on three basic teachings. First is 'naam japo' or repeating the name of God. The second is 'kirat karo', meaning do your work honestly. The third is 'vand chako', meaning share the fruits of your work with everyone.

The Guru Granth Sahib, in Nanak's words, also says:

Jinee naam dhiaee gaye masakath ghall; Nanak, thae mukh oujalee kaethee shuttee naal

'Those who mediate on the Holy name and worked hard;
they are radiant and save others as well' (GGS Ang 388).

Guru Nanak also says: '*Dhuaadhasee daan naam isnaan*' meaning 'on the twelfth day (of the lunar month), give in charity, repeat the Lord's name and purify yourself' (GGS Ang 299). Bhai Gurdas says in Vaars, '*Aan mahaa parasaadh vand khavaiaa*', meaning 'they bring sacred food, distribute it among others and eat'. This captures the spirit of 'vand chako', the third pillar of Sikh teaching.

The teachings are simple and straightforward. They are based on worship of the formless God. The worship is through purification, which is achieved by 'naam', the sacred word, by honest work and by charity. Purity is required to remove the covering of karma due to which we are in bondage and subject to death and rebirth. By following these teachings, we become free or liberated and also enjoy bliss here and now.

Sikh Philosophy

Sikhism is the most recent of the religions that have a sacred text. Many scholars have written about Sikh philosophy. It has some things in common with Hinduism, Buddhism and Jainism, the other religions that originated in India. The core beliefs in karma, rebirth and moksha or liberation are common to all these religions, including Sikhism.

The Guru Granth Sahib refers to them repeatedly. Thus, human beings reap the rewards of their own deeds or suffer their consequences. Karma envelopes the soul and conceals God. Purifying oneself through the divine name is the method of realizing the truth or God. God is formless, the doer and the creator, without any hatred, beyond time, unborn, self-existent and eternal. The concept as laid down in the mool mantar is similar to the Hindu concept of Isvara, who is the formless creator. Sikhism is strongly theistic, in contrast to Jainism and Buddhism. God is also within the human being and can be realized. Guru Nanak said God is neither Hindu nor Muslim. He interacted with many Muslim saints and his constant companion, Mardana, was a Muslim. They visited Mecca as well. The Guru Granth Sahib has verses from Hindu and Muslim saints. It is therefore an inclusive religion.

God is beyond both space and time, yet also manifest in each individual (*hukmai sabko andar*). God is also the creator and watches over the universe (GGS, Ang 8). Thus, God is transcendent and immanent as well as the creator and ruler of the universe. It repeatedly says that God cannot be described. This concept of God is closest to the Visishtadvaita philosophy of Hinduism, though a major difference between them is idol worship.

Epistemologically, the method of gaining God is through the divine name. This theme is repeated several times in the Guru Granth Sahib.

Sikhism does not believe in idol worship or elaborate rituals. At the spiritual and philosophical level, it is against the caste system and treats all people as equal. In practice, some remnants of the Hindu caste system may sometimes be seen, though much weaker than in Hinduism. The idea of *kar seva* or service is strongly ingrained in the practice of Sikhism. Thus, people go and serve in the gurdwara, cleaning, cooking and serving visitors.

Sects in Sikhism

Sikhism says there are *sampardais* or traditions within the religion. Perhaps the earliest were the Udasis, said to have been founded by Sri Chand, who was Guru Nanak's elder son. They emphasized asceticism and lived as monks. For a brief period, they also controlled the Harmandir in Amritsar. However, they are no longer a force and seem to have merged with Hinduism. There were some sects later that were established as rivals to the Gurus. These have also now disappeared. Some major traditions that remain are the Nihang, Nirankari, Namdhari, Nirmala and the mainstream Khalsa.

The Nihangs are a small, armed warrior sect within Sikhism. In early Sikh history, they dominated the army. They were also known as Akali, meaning they were timeless or subject to none but God. Today, Akal has become more mainstream and refers to the Akal Takhts or the religious seats of authority within Sikhism. The Namdhari sect was established in the early nineteenth century. Their name derives from the word naam or sacred word, and means those who wear or hold onto the sacred word. They advocate non-violence, vegetarianism and abstinence from alcohol and tobacco. They have a tradition of living Gurus, which they claim is an unbroken lineage from Guru Nanak. The Nirankari sect was established in the mid-nineteenth century. They wanted to go back to original Sikhism, from which they felt the religion had moved away to some extent. They believe in a lineage of living Gurus, while accepting all the earlier ten Gurus. They also accept the Guru Granth Sahib. They say that the sacred text is not a closed book, but living Gurus can add to it. They live in harmony with the mainstream Khalsa sect. The Nirmala sect emphasized spiritual practices, and their philosophy is aligned to Vedanta in Hinduism. Their leaders also remain celibate like the Udasis. In the twentieth century, mainstream Sikhism and the Nirmala sect drifted apart.

The largest sect by far is the Khalsa Panth established by Guru Gobind Singh, the tenth and last Guru, in 1699. They believe in the first ten Gurus and the Guru Granth Sahib. They forbid the use of tobacco. Over time, five Akal Takhts or seats of temporal power and justice were established in close proximity to a gurdwara. The gurdwara itself is the set of spiritual power. The Takht, headed by a leader called a Jathedar, is the head of temporal power and settles disputes. The Takht also holds cultural events pertaining to the Sikh community, including honouring people for outstanding work. There are five major Akal Takhts. The foremost is the one in Amritsar, established by Guru Har Gobind. There is one at Anandpur, Punjab, the same town where the Khalsa Panth was established by Guru Gobind Singh. Another called Patna Sahib is in Patna, Bihar where Guru Gobind Singh was born. The Takht at Damdama, Punjab, is where Guru Gobind Singh prepared the authentic and final version of the Guru Granth Sahib. The Takht at Nanded, Maharashtra, is where Guru Gobind Singh passed away.

Some Often-Used Sikh Phrases

The term *Satnam wahe Guru* is a sacred mantra. The word *sat* derives from the Sanskrit word for truth, and naam is the sacred name. Satnam refers to God and wahe conveys praise and wonder. Guru again refers to God. So it means truth is God. Another common greeting used today is *Sat Sri Akal*. Sri is an honorific used all over India. The phrase means truth is honourable and timeless.

Guru Gobind Singh also gave a rallying cry for the Khalsas: '*Wahe Guru ji ka Khalsa, wahe Guru ji ki fateh*', meaning 'The Khalsa belongs to God, and victory belongs to God'.

Notes

Sikhism is the most recent of the organized religions with a sacred book. More reliable historical details are available compared to the earlier religions. It is a non-proselytizing religion and has remained relatively small—less than 2 per cent of India's population are Sikhs. Of this, the majority are in India in the state of Punjab. They also reside in the UK and Canada in significant numbers. A large number migrated from Pakistan to India in 1947 after Partition.

Given the history of conflict with the Mughal emperors, even today, many Sikhs are in the Indian Armed Forces. Many are also farmers, and others follow modern professions. They live seamlessly with the rest of society. In the same family, one son might become a Sikh, and another remain a Hindu. Intermarriage between Hindus and Sikhs is common. Many non-Sikhs visit gurdwaras, sometimes regularly. Sikhs are allowed to enter other places of worship, just as Guru Nanak did, but they are not encouraged to worship idols.

In many ways, it is the most practical and simplest of religions, based on a highly spiritual foundation laid by Guru Nanak and later Gurus. The sacred text, the Guru Granth Sahib, may be the only one with verses from so many authors, including saints who were not Sikh but were either Hindus or Muslims. We also see for the first time a religious text saying that the Vedas, Old Testament, the New Testament and the Quran refer to the same God.

7

HINDUISM

Introduction

Hinduism is the oldest religion in the world. The oldest texts, the Vedas, date back to around 1800 BCE. The word 'Hindu' is not found in any of the sacred texts. We find instead the term 'Sanatana Dharma' or the eternal religion. Those who lived on the other side of the river Sindhu called the country Hindustan, the land (or *stan*) across the river Sindhu. Indus is a corrupted form of Sindhu, a river which flows through Kashmir and onward to the plains of Pakistan.

Hinduism has by far the most voluminous set of sacred texts. These include the Vedas, the Upanishads, the Brahma Sutras, the the Six Darsanas or philosophies, the Bhagavad Gita, the eighteen Puranas, the Agama Sastras, other sacred scriptures like the Vedangas, the Upavedas, the eighteen Smritis and other highly regarded texts, and the great epics, the Ramayana and the Mahabharata. The Rig Veda Samhita or mantra portion, which is the first part, has over

10,000 verses. One of the Puranas, the Skanda Purana, has over 80,000 verses. The Ramayana has about 24,000 verses, and the lengthier version of the Mahabharata has about 1,00,00 verses. All of them are in Sanskrit. It is difficult to find a simple summary of Hinduism.

Today, some of the medieval philosophies, including Advaita, Visishtadvaita and Dvaita, are regarded as sacred. For the majority of people, the writings, songs and sayings of the popular Bhakti movement, which did not use Sanskrit, are considered sacred. There is no founder of Hinduism, much like Judaism. But unlike Judaism, there is no comprehensive list of prophets. The rishis or seers of the Vedas and the Upanishads are the earliest teachers in Hinduism. The authors of the Vedic hymns and the Upanishads are largely unknown.

Over the millennia, three texts emerged as the foundational texts. They are the Vedas, of which the Upanishads form the core spiritual teachings and have become popular as Vedanta, the Bhagavad Gita and the Brahma Sutras. They are considered the *prasthana traya* or foundational texts of Hinduism. The Vedas are the oldest, and the other two came soon after that. All later sacred texts defer to the authority of the Vedas, often explicitly in the texts themselves. Any disagreement is resolved by accepting the word of the Vedas.

The Upanishads are called the *shruti prasthana* or the revealed text, and sometimes the *upadesa prasthana* or that which gives the teachings. The Brahma Sutras are the *nyaya prasthana*, or the book that gives the logical basis of the Vedanta or Upanishads. The Bhagavad Gita is sometimes called the *sadhana prasthana*, telling us how the teachings can be put into practice.

The texts can more or less be classified into those with revelation, called Shruti, those with philosophy, called the Darsanas, mythology in the Puranas, rituals in the Agama Sastras and moral and ethical codes of conduct in the Smritis. Sometimes, these different texts also touch upon other aspects of religion—for instance, the Puranas may also have some philosophy. We need to note that other religions do not have such a classification of the sacred texts. All aspects of a religion—revelation, philosophy, mythology, rituals and codes of conduct—are usually contained in the same text.

The Sacred Texts: The Vedas

The Vedas are the most sacred and ancient of the Hindu sacred texts. The word Veda comes from the Sanskrit word *vid*, which means to know. Veda simply means knowledge. The Sanskrit verses in the Vedas are considered revelations of the rishis. They were chanted orally for several centuries before being put down in writing.

Several centuries later, Veda Vyasa, revered today as a guru, split the Veda into four. They are the Rig, Yajur,

Sama and Atharva Vedas. Over the millennia, people have memorized these texts and kept them intact.

Each Veda is further divided broadly into four sections. The first is the Samhita portion, which contains the sacred hymns. These hymns are to the Vedic gods like Indra, Agni, Vayu, Varuna, Usha and so on. The second section is the Brahmana, which gives instructions on various Vedic rituals. These are typically based on the sacred fire into which oblations are given accompanied by the chanting of sacred verses. These Vedic sacrifices or *yajnas* are said to confer material and spiritual blessings on those who attend the worship. There were no temples in the Vedic period for any of the Vedic deities, and there are none today.

The third section are the Aranyakas, which literally means of the forest. It implies that people go into the forest to contemplate. The Aranyakas provide the meaning of the rituals and their deeper significance. The last section in each Veda is the Upanishads, also collectively called the Vedanta. The word Upanishad means to sit down (near a teacher to learn). Vedanta means the end or goal of the Vedas. These are relatively short texts and have no rituals or prayers. They go straight to the question of the meaning of human life, the ultimate reality, whether we as human beings can go beyond sorrow and worldly pleasures and so on. They are in the form of questions and answers. They are also part of the Shruti, the revealed texts. There is no idol worship or reference to any of the Vedic gods or the later Puranic Gods. Western philosophers, Nobel Prize-winning physicists and writers and others have read them with great interest and praised the Vedanta. In India, they are studied even now by serious spiritual seekers around the country. All the later medieval philosophies are based on the Upanishads. They are sometimes called *Veda Sira* or crown of the Vedas.

Providing a summary of the Vedas is challenging because they are very lengthy. What do we emphasize and what do we omit? In the earlier ritual portion, there are some profound phrases and verses. We present a few of them here.

एकं सद्विप्रा बहुधा वदन्ति

'*Ekam Sat, Vipra Bahudavadanti.*'

'The truth is one, the wise call it by various names.' This challenges traditional views on the ritual portion, which say that primitive man worshipped forces of nature like rain, wind, fire, water, earth and so on. This indicates the idea of one truth or God. The Vedic deities are merely lesser manifestations of that. Another verse from the Purusha Suktam, a hymn in the earliest Samhita portion of three of the Vedas, says '*Sahasra shirsha Purushah, sahasraksha sahasrapath*', meaning the One Being with a thousand heads, a thousand eyes and a thousand feet. The language is symbolic and refers to the immanent divine in all beings. Later, the same hymn says,

वेदाहमेतं पुरुषं महान्तम् ।
आदित्यवर्णं तमसःपरस्तात् ।
तमेवं विद्वानमृतं इह भंवति ।

'Vedahametam Purusha mahantam, adityavarnam tamasa parastaat.
Tam eva vidvan, amrutam iha bhavati'

'I have known that Supreme Purusha, brilliant like the Sun, beyond all darkness. By knowing Thou (Purusha) alone, immortality is attained even here.'

These are examples of hymns of revelation even in the earlier ritual section of the Vedas. This does not refer to the physical sun, but to the light seen in revelation. Another verse is '*Aa no bhadrah kratvo yantu visvatah*': let noble thoughts come to us from the whole world. This has a scientific outlook of open-minded acceptance of ideas or knowledge from any source, whether from the scripture or not.

There are speculations about the origin of the universe in the famous hymn of creation called the Nasadiya Suktam in the Rig Veda. It says in part:

Existence was not then, nor non-existence,
The world was not, the sky beyond was neither.

What covered the mist? Of whom was that?
What was in the depths of darkness thick?

Death was not then, nor immortality,
The night was neither separate from day,
But motionless did *That* vibrate
Alone, with Its own glory one—
Beyond *That* nothing did exist.

—Translation by Swami Vivekananda

This can be contrasted with later mythologies in the Puranas about the origin of the universe, or with the Old Testament's Genesis. The Rig Veda does not refer to God or any supernatural force in this hymn. We close with one of the most famous *shanti* or peace mantras from the Yajur Veda.

Om. May peace radiate there in the whole sky as well as in the vast ethereal space everywhere.
May peace reign all over this earth, in water and in all herbs, trees and creepers.
May peace flow over the whole universe.
May peace be in the whole universe.
And may there always exist in all peace and peace alone.
Om. Peace, peace and peace to us and all beings!

—Translation by Swami Abhedananda,
Ramakrishna Vedanta Math

The Vedic hymns have to be understood in the context of those times and how language evolved in those times. The principal means of communication for inner experiences of a spiritual nature back then was through symbols. They are not verses of primitive man worshipping nature with wonder.

The Sacred Texts: The Upanishads

The Upanishads came towards the end of the Vedic period. Unlike the earlier Samhita and Brahmana portions of the Vedas, the Upanishads use less symbolic language and go directly to the question of the meaning of human life, our relationship with any ultimate reality, and how we can go beyond all sorrow. They are much shorter texts. While there are 108 Upanishads available today, there is a reference to 250 of them. The earliest Upanishads came during the closing stages of the Vedic period. Many Upanishads were added over the centuries. However, the most quoted are the ten principal Upanishads that belong to the Vedic period. All of them are much shorter, and two of the principal Upanishads have only twelve and eighteen verses. However, they are full of meaning; several commentaries have been written on them and continue to be written even today.

They usually start with an invocatory prayer. One such prayer is:

ॐ पूर्णमदः पूर्णमिदम् पूर्णात् पूर्णमुदच्यते |
पूर्णस्य पूर्णमादाय पूर्णमेवावशिष्यते ||
ॐ शान्तिः शान्तिः शान्तिः || [1]

Om purnam adah purnam idam purnat purnam udacyate
purnasya purnam adaya purnam evavasisyate
Om shanti shanti shanti

The word *purna* means whole and complete. It means everything, material, mental, living beings and the spiritual reality. The word 'infinity' is often used for purna. The verse means 'That is infinite, this is infinite, infinity comes (or emanates) from infinity. If you take infinity from infinity, then infinity alone remains. Om. Peace, peace, peace.'

Contemplation of this verse helps the mind focus on the study of the Upanishads, which are about the formless ultimate reality, Brahman. Brahman comes from the root word *brih*, which means vast, expanding. Brahman is infinite, eternal, without change, unborn, all-pervasive, self-luminous, beyond space and time. It is *sat-chit-ananda*, or existence, knowledge and bliss. Existence is the nature of the Being, knowledge comes from consciousness and bliss is the effect of love. So Brahman is that Being whose nature is consciousness and love. It is also said that *satyam jnanam anantam brahma*, or truth, knowledge and the infinite is Brahman. While Brahman is the transcendent or cosmic aspect of reality, the words Atman and Purusha are used for the immanent divine that resides in all living beings.

These concepts enable us to understand the contents of the Upanishads. A few of the revelatory verses are given below, which give us a glimpse into the contents. They describe the immanent divine.

'*Atha yadatah paro divo jyotirdeepyate viswatah, prishteswanuttameshuttameshu lokeshvidam vaava, tadyadidamasminnantah Purusho jyotisyaisha*'

'Now that light which shines above this heaven, higher than all, higher than everything, in the highest world, beyond which there are no other worlds, that is the same light which is within man.'

—Chandogya Upanishad 3.13.7,
translated by Max Mueller

It tells us where happiness is:

'*Yo vai bhūmā tatsukhaṃ nālpe sukhamasti bhūmaiva sukhaṃ*'

'That which is infinite is the source of happiness. There is no happiness in the finite. Happiness is only in the infinite.'

—Chandogya Upanishad

It also tells us when we can get to that state:

'Yadā sarve pramucyante kāmā ye'sya hṛdi śritāḥ |
atha martyo'mṛto bhavatyatra brahma samaśnute ||'

'When every desire in the heart of a man has been loosened from its moorings, then this mortal becomes immortal; even here he enjoys Brahman in this human body.'
—The Brihadaranyaka and the Katha Upanishads

So the Upanishads tell us that there is an ultimate reality called Brahman, that the same divinity is within us, that happiness is only in the infinite, and that when desires are loosened, we realize Brahman and go beyond sorrow.

The essence of the Upanishads is said to be in the four Mahavakyas or 'great sayings'. The first is 'Prajnanam Brahma' from the Aitareya Upanishad in the Rig Veda. It literally means 'Consciousness is Brahman'. The next is 'Aham Brahmasmi' from the Brihadaranyaka Upanishad in the Yajur Veda. This means that 'this Self (Atman) is Brahman'. The third is 'Ayam Atma Brahma' from the Mandukya Upanishad in the Atharva Veda. This also means that the Atman is Brahman. The fourth Mahavakya is *'Tat tvam asi'* from the Chandogya Upanishad in the Sama Veda. This means 'you are that (Brahman)'. The teacher is telling his disciple not once, but nine times, that he is Brahman.

Each saying has a set of verses that lead up to it. In the first Mahavakya, the question is what is Brahman? Is it that by which we experience the world through the senses? Is it the faculty of the mind, perception, intellect etc? It says everything in the universe is controlled by Brahman. It ends by saying Consciousness is Brahman.

In the next saying, it symbolically describes creation and asks what the ultimate reality is in all this. It ends by saying that the Self is Brahman. Here, it does not refer to the body, the senses or the mind. It refers to the real Self or Atman within each individual.

In the third, it focusses on the sacred syllable Om. It says Om is all this, it is past, present and future, it is beyond time. Om indeed is Brahman and ends by saying that this Atman in all human beings is Brahman. This is a method of meditation on Om since the description of the sacred syllable helps to take the mind beyond the universe and time.

The last Mahavakya is preceded by verses that culminate in the teacher telling the student 'you are that (Brahman)'. When bees collect nectar from different flowers and mix them, the nectar from one flower is no longer aware that it is separate from others. Similarly, when someone attains the Self, they are not aware that they are separate from others. Whatever is born in the world as animal or insect is not aware where it has come from. That which is the subtlest in all this is the Self. You are that Self. The student asks for further explanation. This idea that everything comes from the Self and is not separate from it is repeated. Each time it ends by the teacher telling the student, 'You are that Self or Brahman'.

Some indications of what Brahman is given repeatedly in the Upanishads. They repeatedly refer to the sacred syllable Om and say it is Brahman. This is the same as the Biblical saying 'In the beginning was the word, the word was with God, and the word was God.' Light as a symbol of Brahman, or rather the first experience of Brahman, is also repeated several times in different Upanishads. Some verses say that Brahman is even beyond that light—where the sun, moon, stars and lightning do not shine. An identical verse of going beyond light is in the exalted utterances of Buddha in the Udana of the Khuddaka Nikaya of the Sutta Pitaka.

Another principal idea is that divinity is immanent or within the human being. For instance, the Mundaka Upanishad says '*antar sarire jyotirmaye hi shubro*', meaning 'in the body is that pure light'. Several Upanishads say this. The most appealing aspect is that of joy or bliss. In the Anandavalli or section of bliss in the Taittiriya Upanishad, a series of verses convey that the bliss of Brahman is infinite and beyond any earthly or heavenly joys. All the Upanishads say that the realization of Brahman leads to supreme bliss.

Some other common themes are meditation as a means of realizing that Brahman, the supreme importance of adhering to truth, and that Brahman is all-pervading. To conclude, the Upanishads say:

1. There is a supreme reality called Brahman. One definition is that It is of the very essence of existence, knowledge and bliss or *'sat-chit-ananda brahma'*. Another definition is that It is truth, knowledge and infinite, *'satyam jnanam anantam brahma'*.
2. Within each living being is the Atman or Purusha. In the Svetasvatara Upanishad, it says *'shrinwantu viswe amritasya putrah'*, meaning 'Listen the world over, you are the children of immortality'. Other Upanishads also say this.
3. This Atman and Brahman are the same. The Mahavakyas also say this.
4. This Atman can be realized by the sincere aspirant; it takes you beyond all sorrow and frees you from the cycle of birth and death.

The Sacred Texts: The Brahma Sutras

This text came just after the Vedic period and precedes the Bhagavad Gita. It is a short, concise text of 555 verses written as sutras or aphorisms. These aphorisms are loaded with meaning, and several commentaries on the Brahma Sutras have been written. The text is also called the Vedanta Sutras or the Bhikshu Sutras, the teaching for monks. It gives a philosophical basis for the revelations in the Upanishads.

The text is very dense and has many subtle arguments. It establishes the final purport of the Upanishads. It says that the Upanishads are an enquiry into Brahman, and that by knowing Brahman, one attains liberation. To establish this, there are arguments to show that all statements in the Upanishads referring to the origin of everything refer to Brahman alone and not to anything else like life, mind, senses, food and so on. It refutes all arguments that say otherwise and establishes that there is a Consciousness behind everything. It negates nihilism and other philosophies that deny any reality and says there is indeed a Reality. It gives a method of realizing Brahman, which is by meditation and discrimination between the real and the unreal. In Hindu philosophy, that which changes or is born, and dies is not real. It may seem real for some time or even a long time, but finally it dissolves like clouds that disappear. Only that which is eternal is real. So meditation on this using Om as a symbol of reality is suggested. It gives some indications that it can be thought of as the origin of everything, or as space, light, a steady flame. This is an ancient technique of focusing the mind and finally stilling it, which automatically reveals Brahman or the Atman. It ends by establishing that the goal in the Upanishads is to know Brahman, which leads to liberation.

The Brahma Sutras, though short, are studied by serious spiritual seekers even today. Philosophically, it gives the ontology and the epistemology of Hinduism—the description of reality and the means of gaining that knowledge. There are other darsanas or philosophies including Nyaya, Vaiseshika, Sankhya, Yoga and Purva Mimamsa. But the Brahma Sutras are given the highest place among them. Among other religions, the sacred texts of Jainism also address these questions, but come to slightly different conclusions. Buddha did not say much about these questions, but the Abhidhamma Pitaka and later Buddhist philosophies also go into these questions and come to yet another set of conclusions. But all religions say that practice is more important than any intellectual comprehension and study.

The Sacred Texts: The Bhagavad Gita

This is the third pillar of the three foundational texts called the *prasthana traya* of Hinduism. It is also a relatively short text of 700 verses within the epic Mahabharata. It is taught by Krishna to his disciple Arjuna. Krishna is considered an avatar or incarnation of God. There is a similar concept in Christianity, where Jesus is the Son of God. Arjuna is a prince and a warrior. The teaching is set in the middle of battlefield, when war is about to begin between Arjuna's side, called the Pandavas, and his cousins, the Kauravas.

The Bhagavad Gita comes soon after the Brahma Sutras. It has several new ideas that were not present in the earlier Vedas and Upanishads. The first is that of a personal god, namely Krishna, who can give liberation. This idea is entirely missing in the Upanishads. The path of devotion or bhakti to a personal god, which leads to liberation, is also new. For the first time, someone stands up and says 'I am God'. Again, this is not there in the Upanishads. Though the Ramayana precedes the Bhagavad Gita and Rama is also considered an avatar, there is no explicit statement by Rama that he is God. Later medieval texts like Yoga Vasishtha and the Adhyatma Ramayana say Rama is an incarnation. But in the original Ramayana, Rama never takes that position himself.

For the first time, the Bhagavad Gita also gives a comprehensive philosophy of Karma Yoga, the path of selfless work, and says this also leads to liberation. Although there are references to selfless work in Upanishads like the Isa, there is no well-developed philosophy there. Karma Yoga is very practical and can be practised by anyone, in any circumstances, whether monk or householder. The Gita is for everyone, not just for monks or those who have renounced the world. This makes it far more appealing than the earlier scriptures.

The Bhagavad Gita also integrates the four principal methods of knowing God. These are:

1. The path of knowledge or Jnana Yoga, which utilizes the intellect and the power of discrimination to arrive at the ultimate truth. The aspirant remains aware and separates the self from the thoughts. This is similar in many ways to some Buddhist methods of meditation, including Vipassana. This is also a principal method in the Upanishads.

2. The path of devotion or Bhakti Yoga, which gives a higher direction to human emotions and turns it into love of God. This love of God is not necessarily for a formless, transcendent God for whom it is difficult to have love, but for a personal god with form and attributes. Through this method also, one can realize God or even the ultimate formless truth. The Jesus prayer and the Sikh 'naam simran' or constant remembrance of the name of God is somewhat similar to this method.

3. The path of meditation or Dhyana Yoga. This is also called Raja Yoga. Here, will power is used to focus the mind and increase concentration on one thought or symbol. This finally leads to stilling of the mind and to knowledge of the Atman. The mind of such a yogi is said to be steady and bright like a flame in a windless place. One of the Buddhist methods called Zen is similar to this, and some point out that Zen is derived from Dhyana.

4. The path of selfless works or Karma Yoga. This is perhaps unique to the Bhagavad Gita. The theory is very

simple. Deep-rooted impressions in the mind, called samskaras, are the result of previous karma or work. Physical work, thinking, feeling, dreaming, imagining and so on are all karmas and they leave impressions in the mind. These samskaras, which are the result of previous karma, obscure the Atman and keep us in ignorance. They also impel us to action, which again leads to further samskaras. Thus we are caught in the wheel of karma, repeated birth and death, subject to joys and sorrows, but never experience permanent peace or bliss. The Gita tells us that it is attachment or clinging that leads to the formation of new impressions. Through detached work, the old impressions are expressed, worked out and resolved without creating new samskaras. Finally, after practising this for a long time, all karmas are exhausted, and we realize the truth within.

The theory of karma is more or less the same in all Indian religions, with slight variations. Hinduism, Buddhism, Jainism and Sikhism tell us how to finally get rid of karma and become free. The philosophies are different, and the methods seem different, but they all start with the fact of karma, which covers up the truth within, and the need to cleanse ourselves of them.

The Gita also has discussions on metaphysics and ontology, about what knowledge is and the difference between knowledge, the knower and the object of knowledge. It also has subtle statements about the manifest and the unmanifest, God with form and attributes and that which is beyond. It does not prescribe one method for all but invites us to choose that which appeals to us. Following one or more of these methods, we can reach the goal of life.

Hindu Philosophy

In Western religion, the word theology is used, but in the Indian religions, the word philosophy is used more often. That is because it touches on various aspects of life and accepts non-theistic doctrines as well.

Hinduism has a highly developed set of philosophical writings. There is no insistence on any one doctrine. While all of them accept the Vedas, they freely gave different interpretations. In other religions, there is either a strict adherence to the founder's words, as in Buddhism, Christianity, Islam and Sikhism, or to a set of founders, as in Judaism and Jainism. In Hinduism, there is no special allegiance to anyone, though different sects within Hinduism are free to adhere to one or the other God, avatar or saint. This has led to a wide variety of philosophies—perhaps the widest of all the religions.

The concept of God is also not defined in a way that all Hindu doctrines accept. In the Abrahamic religions, the concept is monotheism, or one God, and pantheism or worship of different gods through idols and images is forbidden. Among various concepts of God, Hinduism also has one doctrine that is monotheistic and similar to the Abrahamic concept of monotheism.

Before we understand this, we need to understand that in Hinduism, the ultimate reality is not viewed through the lens of monotheism, pantheism and henotheism. In the Hindu view, the monotheism of the Abrahamic religions presumes that God and the world are separate, and that human beings and God are separate. So we pray to God who is different from us. But Hinduism does not accept this at face value. Some of their doctrines say that God resides in the human heart, and another doctrine says that the divine in man is the same as God.

The word God also is used differently in Hinduism. The ultimate reality, as mentioned earlier, is Brahman, formless and infinite. It is unmanifest. God or Isvara as creator and sustainer or Lord of the universe is a manifestation of the creative, dynamic aspect of the unmanifest. The Upanishads and the Gita refer to it. The Gita says 'Beyond the manifest and unmanifest creation, there is yet another eternal unmanifest, that is never destroyed' (BG Chapter 8:20). It refers to that which is beyond space, time and causation. Beings are born and die within space and time. Within this realm, the law of causation also operates—for instance, anything that is born eventually dies. Beyond this space, time and causation is the ultimate reality. In this sense, the Upanishads and the Gita say that Isvara or God as creator and law giver emerges from this highest unmanifest.

Therefore, in the Hindu view, monotheism is nothing but dualism or the doctrine of Dvaita. This means that though there is one God, human beings and the world are separate from It.* This God as creator is manifest. Another doctrine of Visishtadvaita says the ultimate reality has two attributes—living beings and the material universe. In this view, God is both transcendent and immanent. In Advaita or mon-dualism, there are no two things. So God, living beings, the world are all one, and all this manifest is also the same as the unmanifest. No one doctrine of God prevails.

In earlier philosophies, Nyaya, Vaiseshika and Sankhya are silent about God and do not mention any creator or law giver for the universe. The Yoga Sutras of Patanjali mention Isvara's role as the giver of the fruits of action for the aspiring yogi, but not as creator. The most conservative philosophy, namely Purva Mimamsa, emphasizes Vedic rituals as the final goal of life, leading to religious merit. However, it says the Vedas and the world always existed, and the fruits of action are obtained by following the Vedic rituals. So there is no need of God. The later evolution of

---

* 'It' when referring to God is gender-neutral but includes both male and female.

the philosophy started accepting God. The Brahma Sutras accept the role of God as the law giver and creator. The Advaitic interpretation of the Brahma Sutras says that even this concept of God is ultimately not real.

We see a wide variety of philosophies and there is no final word. Just like the innumerable gods and various religious practices, Hinduism leaves it to the individual to accept any of the philosophies. However, it is widely accepted that any method ultimately leads the individual forward on the spiritual path.

Idol Worship and Love of God

Among the world's religions, Hinduism is unique because it sanctions idol worship and also talks of various incarnations of God. No other religions have these two aspects. These concepts developed in the post-Vedic period in the Puranas.

The abstract ideas of the Upanishads no doubt have a universal appeal beyond India. They are based on an intellectual approach to realize a formless and sometimes an attribute-less Reality. However, this appeals only to a small segment of people. The religious impulse the world over is expressed through devotion, reverence and wonder. The human mind is so constructed that it can think only in terms of forms, symbols and words. Again, individuals are attracted to different things even within religion. This is seen in the splitting of all religions, without exception, into various sects. One principal reason is that one approach or philosophy does not appeal to everyone even within a religion.

In India, and particularly in Hinduism, there was a recognition that people needed different approaches to God. In the Puranic period, the concepts of various gods, who never take birth but are nevertheless human in form with attributes like omniscience, power and love, arose. Such gods protect the devotee and give them material and spiritual benefits. There are literally millions of gods and goddesses in Hinduism. But most people understand that behind all these gods, there is only one formless Reality or Truth.

The Puranic gods include Vishnu, Siva and Brahma (not to be confused with the Upanishadic Brahman) and their consorts Lakshmi, Parvati and Saraswati. Brahma is the creator, Vishnu the sustainer and Siva the destroyer or dissolver of the world. In Puranic mythology, the universe goes through repeated cycles of birth and dissolution.

Vishnu is the Immanent God who resides in everything and in all living beings. Siva is transcendent, beyond space and time. Thus, it is Vishnu who incarnates Himself as a human being. Siva does not but can manifest Himself to special devotees or in some persons. Vishnu appeals to those who consider the world as real. Siva, in this sense, appeals to those who seek transcendence. The Divine

Mother or Devi appeals to those who think of God as full of power and energy. This is merely illustrative, but the idea is that there is perhaps a psychological truth behind various gods and goddesses. Worshipping them is easier for people of that temperament.

Along with the Puranic lore there are the Agama Sastras, which lay down the way temples are constructed, idols made and consecrated, and how worship is done. In practice, many temples do not follow the detailed rules laid down in the Agamas. Simple worship is considered enough.

Bhakti literature also includes the Narada Bhakti Sutras, a major text on devotion. This and other texts tell us to establish a personal relationship with God. From a God who is far away in some heaven, all-powerful, God becomes a master, a friend, a parent, even a child or a lover. The psychology here is that it is easier to approach God, love Him or Her, if we establish a personal relationship. In medieval times, several saints wrote songs that illustrate this. Ramprasad considered himself a child of Kali, the Mother Goddess. He challenges her and says he is not her weak, premature child; he has her sacred name and will sue her in court if she does not reveal herself to him! Meera considered herself a lover of Krishna and said she remembered him with every breath. Ravidas considered himself a servant of God. Tyagaraja considered Rama to be his saviour, to whom he had surrendered. There are literally hundreds of songs in every Indian language. This helped to spread the basic ideas of Hinduism to all people.

This unique idea in Hinduism brings God closer to anyone of a devotional temperament. It also says that God can take any form he pleases. In the same family, you might find people worshipping different gods. It builds a kind of acceptance of all other gods and of people who worship other gods. Since people have personal preferences, idol worship of a personal god gives individuals more choice.

At the same time, some people are bewildered by so many gods and, even within Hinduism, may not believe in them. This is also accepted. God is also not worshipped only for spiritual benefit, but also for material gain.

Incarnations of God

This is also a unique Hindu concept. God takes birth occasionally for the good of the world. Christianity has the concept of only one Incarnation, Jesus Christ. Other religions do not believe in this idea. However, in Hinduism, there are many Incarnations.

There are two ways of understanding this idea. One is through mythology and the other is through the spiritual power that an Incarnation manifests. Mythology tells us that there were either ten Incarnations of Vishnu, or according to another Purana, twenty-four avatars. The ten avatars include fish, tortoise, boar, Narsingha (half man, half lion) and five others in human form, namely Vamana, Parasurama, Rama, Krishna, Balarama and the yet-to-manifest Kalki avatar. In some Puranas, Balarama is replaced by Buddha. Though Buddha rejected the Vedas, and the Puranas accept them, some added Buddha to their list of Incarnations. The Buddhists themselves do not consider Buddha to be an Incarnation. The list of twenty-four avatars is in the Bhagavat Purana which lists sages like Kapila, Dattatreya, the twin sages Nara-Narayana and others as partial incarnations of God. It goes on to add that there can be more as well.

The idea behind the Avatar is more important. The Avatar is identified completely with Brahman. Swami Vivekananda says, 'Avataras are Kapâlamochanas, that is, they can alter the doom of people . . . One who can alter the doom of people is the Lord. No Sadhu, however advanced, can claim this unique position.' God is the *phaladata*, who gives the fruits of our actions. The Avatar can also do this. The Avatar can raise the consciousness of people. Krishna reveals his Divine form to Arjuna in the Bhagavad Gita, which includes the whole universe.

Devotees also worship the avatar for centuries. This does not happen in the case of ordinary saints. Vivekananda refers to Krishna and says, 'Five thousand years have passed and he has influenced millions and millions.' He called Buddha 'the most gigantic spiritual wave ever to burst upon human society', and about Jesus, he says, '. . . the three years of his ministry were like one compressed, concentrated age, which it has taken nineteen hundred years to unfold'.[1] Avatars can also redeem the fallen. Rama is called *patita pavana*, one who purifies the sinner. Jesus also forgave the sins of many. Krishna says, 'Surrender to me, and I shall redeem you of all sins, do not fear.'[2]

The Caste or Varna and Jati System

This is a unique aspect of Hinduism. In modern terminology, it is called caste, but the original word is *varna*, which classified people based on their temperament or aptitude for different types of work. In the most sacred texts, namely the Vedas and the Upanishads, there are stray references to varna. The Purusha Suktam in the Rig Veda mentions that Brahmins emerged from the mouth of the Purusha, Kshatriyas from the arms, Vaishyas from the thighs and Shudras from the feet. This is part of a series of verses constructing a mythology of how the earth and living beings were created, and how animals, humans, plants and so on were created. It can be considered mythology or as literally true depending on one's point of view.

The Shukla Yajur Veda (XXVI. 2) explicitly says that all persons, irrespective of their varna, are qualified to learn the Vedas:

यथेमां वाचं कल्याणीमावदानि जनेभ्यःब्रह्मराजन्याभ्यां शूद्राय चार्याय च सुवाय चारणाय ॥

Yathemaqm vacham kalyanima vadani janebhyah, brahma, rajanyabhyam, sudraya cha aryaya cha swaya charanaya

It means 'May I speak the sacred word to the masses of the people (janebhya) to the Brahmana, Kshatriya, to the Shudra and the Arya and to our own men and the strangers.' This includes all people.

In the Chandogya Upanishad, one of the most sacred of the Principal Upanishads with one of the Mahavakyas, the teacher accepts Satyakama Jabala as a student. He is an illegitimate child, considered an outcaste or lower than the lowest caste, in later times. His mother Jabala told him that as she was a servant maid in several households, she was not sure who his father was. The young boy truthfully reports this to the teacher, who very gladly accepts him because he tells the truth. The teacher says that he who can tell such a truth is a Brahmin. Here, a Brahmin is defined by adherence to truth, not by birth.

The Bhagavad Gita also refers to the four varnas. It says that the four varnas are based on *svabhāva-prabhavaih-gunaih* or 'qualities influenced or determined by one's nature'. Even later, in the time of Buddha, the word Brahmin is used several times. It refers to learned persons. In some places, Buddha says that those who follow the teachings and gain true wisdom are sages, ascetics, Brahmins. Though Buddha rejected the varna system, he uses the word Brahmin several times.

At the same time, later texts like the Manu Smriti have a few verses giving a low status to the Shudra caste and prescribing punishment for transgressions like learning the Vedas. This is clearly against the Shukla Yajur Veda verse mentioned earlier.

Thus in the Vedas, Upanishads and the Gita, it seems that in ancient times, the varna system may not have been based on birth. It was most probably based on the aptitude and temperament of the individual. Over time, it got entrenched as a birth-based system. Later, the *jati* system evolved in which various sub-divisions based on work arose. Thus, there were carpenters, washermen, cobblers, fishermen, stone workers, farmers, dairy farmers, sheep and goat herders and so on.

There are several sides to the debate on varna and jati. Those who take a purely spiritual view of Hinduism say that these divisions have little to do with religion; they are merely social constructs. Another group rejects this, points to Scheduled Caste persons being prevented from temple entry and says that caste is very much a part of religion. For many with this view, a caste-less society is required, and they criticize the Hindu religion. Then there are those who accept that there are divisions but say that this is natural and such divisions exist in all countries. Even those who convert from Hinduism to other religions face discrimination due to caste.

Vivekananda says of this system:

'Now the original idea of Jati was this freedom of the individual to express his nature, his Prakriti, his Jati, his caste . . . Not even in the latest books is inter-dining prohibited; nor in any older books is inter-marriage forbidden . . . Any crystallized custom or privilege or hereditary class in any shape really prevents caste (Jati) from having its full sway.'[3]

He clearly says it cannot be based on birth but has to be based on the freedom of the individual to choose his or her vocation in life. Today, all forms of discrimination based on caste is forbidden by law.

The Esoteric Aspects of Hinduism

Hinduism has developed several spiritual methods that lead to enlightenment. These methods are usually passed down from guru to disciple. Only an illumined person can be a guru. Mere knowledge of the sacred texts is not enough. The guru initiates the disciple into the spiritual life. This initiation eventually bears fruit over time as the disciple follows the spiritual practices taught by the guru, which leads to enlightenment.

This is common to all Indian religions, and perhaps the mystic traditions in the Abrahamic religions also. However, in Hinduism, there are several spiritual traditions that are alive today. Each has separate rituals, mantras and practices. Thus, in the north, there are the Kabir panthis who follow the teachings of the saint Kabir, who believed in the formless God. There are the Ramanand Sampradayis, who believe in worshipping Rama as God. The Vaishnav sect in Bengal worships Krishna and believes that the saint Chaitanya was a manifestation of Krishna. There is a tradition of Siva among the Saiva Siddhantas in the south and the Lingayats who worship Siva as a *linga* or symbol and wear it around their neck. They do not strictly accept the Vedas and say that Siva resides in the body, and so we should look after the body and not abuse it. The Naga sect of monks remain nude. The Nath Sampradaya follows Vedanta. The Dasanami sect of monks follow Advaita. There are monks in the Visishtadvaita and Dvaita sects. Modern-day spiritual gurus do not belong to any particular tradition.

The Agama Sastras speak of mantra, *yantra* and tantra. There is a whole science of the mantra. One definition of mantra is '*mananat trayate, iti mantra*', or that which protects the mind is mantra. It is a set of sacred syllables passed down from the guru to the earnest spiritual seeker. The Upanishads and the Vedas use the syllable Om. Two of the well-known ones are Om Namah Shivay for Siva, also called the five syllable *panchakshari* mantra, and Om Namo Narayanaya for Vishnu or Narayana. Later, other mantras for various gods and avatars emerged. Yantra is a diagram used in worship. One well-known one is the Sri Chakra puja done using this diagram, where God is worshipped as the mother. Tantra is defined as '*tanyate vistaryate jnanam anena iti tantram*', or that which spreads knowledge to all people.

All these practices take us from where we are and move us forward in the spiritual life. Some of the practices lead us gradually away from worldly life and enjoyments to the spiritual life. Some emphasize renunciation. The various practices, rituals, mantras and symbols appeal to some aspect of our psychology and become attractive. However, many practices are not esoteric, and consist of simple prayers, songs and meditation.

The basic underlying idea in Hinduism, of different paths for different temperaments, is found in all these methods of reaching the goal.

Common Practices and Teachings

At first, it seems that anything goes in Hinduism. You can believe in God or not, you can believe in any form of God, you can follow any doctrine or philosophy or any set of practices. It is not as arbitrary as it seems. Behind this, there are some common things, no matter what one's belief is or which path one follows. The need for purity of mind is common across all paths. This is attained by control of the mind and the senses. Moral and ethical teachings or dharma must be followed, no matter which path one follows. This includes, for instance, avoiding all negative actions like lying, stealing, sensual indulgence and selfish actions, and cultivating positive virtues like friendliness, benevolence, charity or *daanam*. The ego has always to be kept in check. The reason is simple—the obstruction to the truth is attachment to the body, mind and senses, and to the ego. Without loosening their hold, one cannot make spiritual progress. For those who believe in God, surrendering the results of all our actions to God and being humble before Him is taught. For those who do not believe in God, detachment from the world and from the body, mind and senses is required.

The various paths are many ways of reaching the same goal of spiritual awakening and enlightenment.

The Essential Bases of Hinduism

Hinduism is based on the Vedas and Upanishads. Vivekananda says, 'The only point where, perhaps, all our sects agree is that we all believe in the scriptures—the Vedas . . . Whatever be his philosophy or sect, everyone in India has to find his authority in the Upanishads . . . And the law is that wherever these Puranas and Smritis differ from any part of the Shruti, the Shruti must be followed, and the Smriti rejected.' Buddhism and Jainism, which rejected the Vedas, were not accepted within the religion, but all other differing philosophies and creeds that accepted the Vedas found a place in Hinduism. In practice however, there is no conflict today between these religions.

The Upanishads say that there is an ultimate reality called Brahman, which is formless, eternal, unchanging, unborn, un-decaying, self-luminous, full of bliss, beyond space and time, of the very nature of truth and knowledge, and infinite. Later philosophies disagreed on whether the world was real or not. Advaita holds that the world is perceived through the mind and senses only. In the fully illumined state, the world is unreal or changing. Other philosophies say that the world is either an aspect of Brahman or separate from it. The world as separate from Brahman is similar to the monotheistic concept of the Abrahamic religions. There is a statement in the Chandogya Upanishad that says 'sarvam khalvidam Brahma', which means everything is Brahman.

All living beings have the Atman, the spiritual essence of all sentient beings. This includes not only human beings but all sentient beings. Human birth gives us the opportunity to realize the Atman. This Atman and Brahman are related. According to Advaita, they are one and the same. The principal argument is that the Atman is eternal and infinite. Since there cannot be two infinities,

Atman and Brahman are identical. Visishtadvaita holds that the Atman is identical to Brahman but separate from it. A drop of water is essentially the same as the ocean but much smaller. Dvaita holds that the Atman is at best a reflection of Brahman and is eternally separate from it. In any case, all philosophies agree with the Upanishads, that knowledge of the Atman leads to liberation.

The various gods and goddesses in Hinduism are different manifestations of that One Reality. The Rig Veda says 'ekam sat, vipra bahuda vadanti', or truth is one, sages call it by different names. The concept of the avatar is unique to Hinduism. In practice, the avatars are human, mainly the Rama, Krishna and Narsingha avatars. People worship them and there are temples dedicated to these avatars.

Advaita philosophy does not accept this concept since it says 'brahma satya, jagat mithya', meaning that Brahman is real and the world or manifestation is unreal. Since the avatar is also a manifestation in this world, Advaita does not accept the avatar. However, in practice, it says that worship of the avatar leads to liberation as you go from the personal to the impersonal, and from form to formlessness.

Like other Indian religions, Hinduism is also based on the idea of karma, which leads to an endless cycle of birth and death, and of final liberation or moksha.

The underlying theme is always acceptance of all different ways of reaching God. In practice, there have been quarrels between different sects of Hinduism. But everyone accepts that all paths lead to the same God. This acceptance of all gods and doctrines is built into the very fabric of Hinduism. The same person prays to different gods and accepts that in reality, there is only one God. This spills over to the acceptance of other religions. The first Christians to come to India were St Thomas the Apostle and some of his followers. They successfully established Christianity in south India. Jews came to India and established synagogues in Kerala. The first Muslims came by sea to Kerala and it is said that one mosque was established in 629 CE, when the Prophet Mohammad was still alive. There were conflicts over the years, but nothing compared to the centuries of war during the Crusades.

Notes

Hinduism is the dominant religion in India, with about 80 per cent of the population being Hindu. A little over 5 per cent of Hindus live in other countries. It is the world's third largest religion after Christianity and Islam. It is a non-proselytizing religion and does not actively convert people. However, Hinduism continues to attract people from around the world who want to lead a spiritual life or seek enlightenment.

Historically, Hinduism faced some challenges. The first one might have been internal. There were many doctrines and they disagreed with each other. By the time of the Bhagavad Gita, we see Krishna saying that those who follow the Vedic rituals can at best go to a (temporary) heaven and have to be born again. He teaches us to follow the spiritual path that leads to liberation. Perhaps there was an overemphasis on Vedic rituals at that time.

The next challenge was from Buddhism, a proselytizing religion. Both Jainism and Buddhism rejected the Vedic rituals and emphasized Ahimsa or non-violence. There was an over emphasis on Vedic rituals, which were controlled by Brahmins and back then, also involved animal sacrifices. Buddha opened the doors of his religion to all people irrespective of their caste or social status and rejected Vedic rituals. Within a few centuries of Buddha, a vast majority of the population had converted to Buddhism. Buddhism came to be dominated by large numbers of monks, some of whom may not have been suited for a celibate life. This led to an inevitable decline. Meanwhile, the influence of the Brahmins had declined. As a reaction, the Vedic religion based on rituals was being revived, although animal sacrifice was abandoned.

It was at this time that Adi Sankaracharya, through his philosophical works, re-established the spiritual ideal in the Vedic religion. Buddhism declined, but so did the ritual aspects of Hinduism. It was first replaced by the Vedantic doctrine of Advaita. This laid a stronger intellectual foundation for Hinduism, but perhaps appealed only to a small set of intellectually inclined people. The Bhakti movement of saints all over India took place, with an emphasis on devotion to a personal god. It was not based on the Vedic ritual form of worship, but on temple and idol worship, as we see in modern-day India. Ramanujacharya established the Visishtadvaita doctrine and Madhvacharya, the Dvaita doctrine. Other doctrines were also established.

Meanwhile, the next challenge came from invaders from Central Asia. The Bhakti movement, the songs and sayings of the saints and the work of the various acharyas and writers helped preserve Hinduism. Later, the colonizing Europeans, including the Portuguese, Dutch, French and British, came and established their rule. There were serious attempts at converting people to Christianity.

In spite of these challenges, external and internal, the core of Hinduism has remained intact. That core is spirituality. The forms and the rituals may have changed over the millennia, but the fundamental truths in the ancient scriptures are accepted even today. In fact, they started being accepted outside India as well from the nineteenth century onwards.

All these challenges have perhaps strengthened the religion, forcing it to introspect and improve itself in practice. While no changes were required at the spiritual level, practices and rituals were modified, and there were efforts to expand its core spiritual appeal to all people. With its wide variety of philosophies, practices, gods, goddesses and a continuous stream of saints, it offered everyone a path of their choice. It does not condemn anyone to eternal hell for not believing in the religion. The Rig Veda in 1.164.39 says that merely knowing the Veda is not enough:

ऋचो अक्षरे परमे व्योमन् यस्मिन्देवा अधि विश्वे निषेदुः ।
यस्तं न वेद किमृचा करिष्यति य इत्तद्विदुस्त इमे समासते ॥

'In the highest imperishable heaven where all the gods reside, and where there are the Rig Vedic verses, what use are these verses to one who does not know the Highest? Only those who know That (highest reality) are satisfied.'

Vivekananda says, 'Of all the scriptures of the world, it is the Vedas alone which declare that the study of the Vedas is secondary. The real study is that by which we *realise* the Unchangeable». And that is neither reading, for believing, nor reasoning, but superconscious perception, or Samadhi.'[4]

The underlying spirit is best embodied in the two verses from the Rig Veda:

'*ekam sat, vipra bahuda vadanti.*'

Truth is one, sages call it by various names, and

'*Aa no bhadrah kratvo yantu visvatah*'

Let noble thoughts come to us from every side.

8

HARMONY OF WORLD RELIGIONS

May He who is the Ahura-Mazda of the Zoroastrians, Buddha of the Buddhists, the Holy One of the Jews, the Father in Heaven of the Christians, Allah of the Muslims and Brahman of the Hindus, lead us from darkness to light, from death to immortality.

Introduction

Any search for harmony among religions has to focus on the sacred texts of the religions. Social norms, customs, rituals, modes of dress and the kinds of food eaten vary across countries and religions. These do not form the core of any religion. Each religion has many scholars and priests with different interpretations of their religion. This may be valuable but could sometimes differ from the scriptures. The various sects within any religion do not differ on the core spiritual teachings or on the sacred texts. They all agree that the founder is the highest authority or teacher. Their differences are on theological or philosophical issues, or on the relative emphasis of one or the other aspect of practice. Sometimes, sects are formed by leaders who disagree with other leaders. Therefore, here we do not focus on later writings but on the original teachings of the founders or the most sacred texts.

There is also a tendency to take a partial view of a religion or quote one or the other extract from a scripture and form conclusions about the entire religion. For instance, some non-Hindus say that there is too much superstition or blind faith, and that some rituals are strange. They cannot relate to idol worship. Some others ask: why is there so much violence in the Ramayana and the Mahabharata, and why are so many gods and avatars shown killing demons and bad people? All this is true, but this is not the essential aspect of Hinduism. It was and still is a serious spiritual search for God or the ultimate truth. The rituals and stories are not the core teaching in the most sacred texts, the Upanishads and the Bhagavad Gita. Similarly, quotes from other religious text apparently exhorting violence are used to denigrate the religion. This is a partial view. The entire scripture must be understood to extract the essence. Proselytizing religions are criticized for 'saving souls' by conversion, or for claiming superiority over other religions. However, the founder's essential teachings are not about conversion or superiority. They are about how to lead a better life.

This type of mutual bickering or conflict arises from a focus on the social, political and external aspects of a religion. No harmony can be found here. Vivekananda says, 'I am a Hindu. I am sitting in my own little well and thinking that the whole world is my little well. The Christian sits in his little well and thinks the whole world is his well. The Mohammadan sits in his little well and thinks that is the whole world.'[1]

The greatest barrier to evolving any harmony is centuries of conflict. Vivekananda says, 'Sectarianism, bigotry, and its horrible descendant, fanaticism, have long possessed this beautiful earth. They have filled the earth with violence, drenched it often and often with human blood, destroying civilization and sent whole nations to despair.' This often makes some people atheistic and they reject religion itself.

However, the overwhelming majority around the world believe either in God or in a higher spirit. So religious differences have to be resolved not by rejecting religion, but by a better understanding of all religions. As mentioned earlier, this has to be found in the sacred scriptures, not by taking a partial view, but by grasping the core of the teachings. Sri Ramakrishna, a nineteenth century Indian saint, said, 'Scriptures contain sugar mixed with sand. It is very difficult to take out only the sugar. Therefore, one should hear the essence of a scripture.'

The Common Bases of Religions

All religions that have survived for centuries or millennia have one thing in common. They all have a set of sacred texts. These texts preserve the basic tenets of the religion and ensure that it survives and grows. The different religions are so many expressions in various languages and symbols of a fundamental search for deeper meaning in life. We discuss some points of similarity, and some apparent points where they differ. We find similarity in the revelations and in the moral and ethical teachings— similarity of revelations in the sense that they are all considered to be either from God or from some other higher, deeper or inner source. They are not from the intellect, mind or the senses.

Revelations of the Founders

All religions stake their claim on revelation. The founder or set of founders are said to have seen or realized super sensory truths, either from God or from some other source. Jainism and Buddhism accept revelation but do not say it comes from God. Moses, Jesus, Mohammad, Buddha,

Mahavira, Guru Nanak and the Vedic rishis all received revelations. Based on that, they taught others.

Revelations are of various types. For instance, in the Torah, God sometimes indicates His presence by a burning bush or a voice. He gives direct commands or teachings. He either performs miracles or gives the prophet the power to perform miracles. Sometimes, the revelation is about future events. In the case of the Prophet Mohammad, his revelations or *wahy* came through the angel Gabriel, but directly conveyed the words of God. Mohammad merely placed these teachings before his followers. However, there are references to inner mystical experiences as well. For instance, his ascent to the highest heaven, where he comes in close proximity with Allah, is a mystical experience. In the case of Jesus, we do not have any direct teachings that God gave him, but his teachings are considered to be of divine origin. We infer that Jesus had revelations based on the miracles he performed, the spiritual power he exhibited and his teachings. In the case of Mahavira, Buddha and Guru Nanak, the revelations are mystic experiences of God or higher truths. The same is true of the rishis of the Vedic period. The Upanishads contain several verses that are the outcome of revelation or a mystic experience. All these revelations transform the individual, who becomes wise, joyful and full of compassion. They receive an inner command or a command from God to teach.

Other than the direct commands and teachings, the inner mystical experience of the prophets can be inferred from the sacred texts or authentic biographies. In the Torah, there is an experience of seeing light, and the prophets are struck with awe and wonder whenever they receive a revelation. Jesus says, 'I am the Light of the world'. Jesus also has the power to show revelations to others. For instance, he appears after his crucifixion to Peter and others. This revelation refers to light. Mohammad heard from Allah that 'He (Allah) is nearer than the vein on your neck' (Quran 50:16). It also says, 'We have sent down to you a clear Light.' (Quran 4:174) The word light is used several times in the Quran. All the religions that arose in India talk of light and the inner mystical experiences of the founders.

The process of gaining revelation is also interesting. All founders, without exception, had to struggle hard for illumination. Moses, Jesus and Mohammad fasted and prayed, sometimes for a month or forty days at a stretch, in isolation. Moses fasted for forty days on Mount Sinai before he got a revelation. Jesus goes into the desert and fasts for forty days and forty nights. Mohammad went into the cave of Hira and fasted for twenty days before he got his first revelation. We do not have information on what else they did during this period. All the Indian religions also talk of some austerity, either of body or mind or both. This includes fasting and controlling the unruly mind and making it calm. Thus, Guru Nanak, Mahavira, Buddha and the Vedic rishis went through long periods of struggle before they gained illumination. Apart from fasting, controlling one's desires is also prescribed. The need to be humble and avoid pride and arrogance is stressed in all religions. Judaism says '*Kedoshim tihyu*'—you shall be holy. The Quran says, 'But as for him who fears to stand before his Lord, and restrains his soul from evil desires, heaven shall surely be his home.' The Guru Granth Sahib says, 'Within the body reside five enemies—desire, anger, greed, attachment and ego.' The foundation of Buddhism in the Four Noble Truths is to give up clinging to the impermanent joys of this world. Jainism says that desire is the root cause of misery. Hinduism says that when the desires are loosened, the individual gains immortality. The ego is considered the final barrier to revelation and has to be done away with.

It is in the deeper mystical or spiritual practices that are said to lead to enlightenment that we find greater commonality. 'Be still and know that you are God' is from the Old Testament. Hindu, Jain and Buddhist practices also aim to still the mind. To love God with all one's heart, soul and strength requires great mental control and focus on one idea. That itself stills the mind.

Thus revelation, and the process of gaining it, are common across religions. Details do vary, based on culture, language and custom. But there some common elements. The contents of the revelation also seem different. We examine later whether they are contradictory or complementary.

The Spiritual Bases of Religions

All religions declare that there is something spiritual in human beings. The word ruah is used in the Old Testament for the spirit, which is in us. Genesis calls it the 'breath of life' (Genesis 6:17). In the book of Job it says 'This same breath of the Almighty is the spirit of wisdom and understanding in us' (Job 34:14-15). In Christianity also, the holy spirit enters Mary when she gives birth to Jesus. The same holy spirit enters John the Baptist. In the Quran, Allah says of human beings 'I have fashioned him in perfection and have breathed into him of My Spirit.' The Indian religions also say the same. Hinduism says that the Atman, or the holy spirit is in all human beings. The Guru Granth Sahib in Sikhism says the commander is inside everyone 'hukmai sabko andar'. Jainism refers several times to the soul which evolves and finally becomes liberated. Buddhism is the only religion that does not accept a soul but does talk of the individual attaining nirvana.

Moral and Ethical Teachings

All religions, without exception, ask to us follow ethical precepts. They emphasize love, compassion, mercy and prohibit actions like killing, stealing, sexual misconduct, telling lies and cheating, and teach us not to hate, be jealous or harm others. The Ten Commandments in Judaism are all ethical teachings. Jesus Christ teaches us to love and serve everybody. He explicitly says that the two greatest commandments are 'Thou shalt love the Lord thy God with all thy heart, soul and mind . . . thou shalt love thy neighbour as thyself' (Mathew 22:37-39). Islam repeatedly uses the word zakat or charity and asks us to give to the poor, the needy and help those who are suffering. Hinduism asks us to treat the guest as God *atithi devo bhava'*, and to treat the whole world as our family *'vasudhaiva kutumbakam'*. Buddha says we should work for the welfare of all, for the happiness of all, and out of compassion for the world, *'bahujana hitaya, bahujana sukhaya, lokanumpaya'*. Sikhism says share the fruit of your work with everyone, *'vand chako'*. One of the vows in Jainism is *'daan'* or charity.

The psychology behind this is simple. By not following moral and ethical teachings, we eventually disturb our mind and become unhappy. However, compassion, forgiveness and charity when done in the right spirit elevate the mind and give happiness.

The theistic religions without exception tell us to love God. Judaism and Christianity explicitly tell us to love God. As mentioned earlier, the first commandment in Judaism and Christianity is to love god with all our heart, soul and mind. Islam also says, 'If you sincerely love Allah, then follow me; Allah will love you and forgive your sins. For Allah is All-Forgiving, Most Merciful' (Quran 3:31, Surah Ali Imran). In Hinduism, the Narada Bhakti Sutras define devotion as intense love of God. This love of God gives peace and joy and can eventually lead to liberation. Sikhism also preaches love of God.

Jainism and Buddhism, the two religions that do not derive their moral or ethical teachings from God, ask us to cultivate love, compassion and kindness for all beings. Buddha uses the words *metta* (kindness) and *karuna* (compassion) repeatedly. In a sense, love of God is redirected in Buddhism and Jainism to love and compassion for all beings.

All religions ask us to purify our minds, which means removing all negative thoughts and controlling unruly desires. The pure mind is not agitated. According to Hinduism, the pure mind experiences the divine. This is similar to Christ's teaching 'Blessed are the pure in heart, for they shall see God.'

Pride and vanity have to be given up. In Judaism, the Ecclesiastes use the word vanity several times, and tells us to give it up. The Book of Proverbs also says that pride comes before a fall. Genesis refers to pride as a deadly sin. Jesus Christ teaches us several times to be humble. Islam also tells us to give up pride and surrender to Allah. The Indian religions are similar. Buddhism and Jainism clearly say that the ego is the barrier to knowledge of the ultimate truth. Sikhism and Hinduism also tells us to be humble.

The moral and ethical teachings of all religions are very similar. By following them, society becomes harmonious and peaceful. Without that, the law of the jungle would prevail and society would be full of strife and conflict. At the same time, such teachings help the individual to lead a peaceful and happy life.

Complementary Aspects of Different Religions

While we see something common in revelation and moral teachings, the other three aspects of religion, namely mythology, philosophy and rituals, are different. Clearly, all religions, even those without a written religious text, evolved myths about creation, about ancient times, about God or gods. These myths are shared by people and create some kind of bonding. All mythologies, without exception, serve one primary purpose. They reinforce faith in the religion or the founder. There seems to be a primeval need for us as human beings to belong to something that is grand, great or inspiring. For the Jews, it is the idea of being God's chosen people. The Torah goes back to ancient times, the suffering of the Jews and how, with God's grace, they finally triumph. For Christians, the idea of Jesus as the only Son of God is very appealing. He gave his life for us, and through him we can get salvation. Jesus is born of immaculate conception, performs many miracles that were never seen before, resurrects himself and is even able to show himself in dazzling light to his disciples at that time. This serves to strengthen faith in Jesus and the religion. For Islam, the Quran is the perfect book, and Mohammad the last and most perfect Prophet. There are stories about his childhood that are miraculous. The Quran has the story of Mohammad's ascent to heaven. First, he goes on a winged horse from Mecca to Jerusalem. Then he ascends to heaven with the help of the angel Gabriel. On the way, he sees all the other prophets, including Abraham, Moses and Jesus. Going further, he arrives alone in the presence of the dazzling light that comes from Allah. It implies that no one had gone that far. In India, the eighteen Puranas in Hinduism, totalling several hundreds of thousands of verses, are full of myths. One constant theme is that God protects us if we are devoted to him. He also destroys evil to protect good people. However, God also pardons and redeems sinners. It serves to give a sense of security to people, and invites them to pray to God and get peace of mind. Jainism has stories about the lives of the Tirthankaras, who were all great, performed superhuman feats and sometimes performed miracles. Buddhist folklore talks about the earlier twenty-three Buddhas, about the previous lives of Buddha in the Jataka tales and also about miraculous events in the life of Buddha. Celestial beings come to learn from him; vain, ignorant gods come to him only to be subdued. It increases faith in Buddha. Sikh literature is recent, but it also has hagiographical accounts of the life of Guru Nanak.

Though the stories are different, they have only one purpose: to increase faith and reverence for the founder or the religion. The parables are often about the victory of good over evil, either due to God's intervention or as a result of following the moral and ethical teachings. The two most ancient religions, Judaism and Hinduism, both have the myth of an ancient flood that nearly destroyed the world. God saves the world. Both religions also have myths of creation. The details of the myths vary, but the underlying message is that God is the creator, is all-powerful and someone whom we should be in awe of and worship.

Rituals of course vary widely. Done in the right spirit and in proportion, they help give structure to religious and even spiritual practices. This is especially true for the beginner. For instance, prayer is common to all religions. Even in Buddhism and Jainism, there are mental prayers before meditation. These prayers may not be to God, but for peace of mind, for the strength to follow the path and so on. But how to pray? How do we worship? Rituals help some people to pray and worship effectively. Bathing, chanting or repeating the sacred texts, kneeling or prostrating, facing a particular direction, the use of light or incense and so on help focus the mind. The rituals vary across religions, but they all help to focus the mind.

Praying to a monotheistic, formless God without ritual might be difficult for many people.

Philosophy

By philosophy, we mean the writings that explain the original sacred texts. In Christianity and the western world, the word theology is used. With respect to the Indian religions, the word philosophy is used. In the sense we use it here, it includes metaphysics, theories about God, the ultimate goal of human life, what happens after death and the relationship between man, the world and God. Discussions about what reality is (God, universe, human beings, life, existence, etc.) are called ontology, but we include them here in this section. For the sake of simplicity, we also include the method of reaching the goal of human life or of gaining knowledge, often called epistemology.

The central concept in most religions is God. Only Jainism and Buddhism do not have a concept of God, except perhaps to either say it is irrelevant or that God does not exist.

Concepts of God

God is a central concept in most religions.

We try to summarize various concepts of God. A western classification is monotheism versus polytheism—

one God verses many. The Abrahamic religions are all monotheistic, with only one God, which is formless. God is the creator and lord of the universe. Such a God has attributes—omniscience, omnipotence, dispenser of justice, rewards and punishments, merciful, full of love and so on.

According to the Indian religions, God as creator is 'dualistic' in the sense that God is separate from the world and living beings, and not immanent in them. Pantheism, on the other hand, says God is immanent in the universe and pervades it. In the Hindu view, all the various gods and goddesses are manifestations of various aspects of the One God. Hinduism also has the concept of a formless, attribute-less God or ultimate reality called Brahman. This is beyond space, time and causation and is transcendent. Hinduism does not have one concept of God. It incorporates all concepts of God in the various philosophies it has.

Jainism says the world and living beings have always been there. In their concept, reality has several aspects, including soul, matter and time. So there is no need for God to create anything. It is explicitly atheist. In monotheistic religions, the world was created at some point in time by God. One key point here is that reality has different aspects according to this view—God, matter, living beings. If they always existed, there is no need for God, as the Jains say, and if they are created, then God is the creator. There is a different concept in Advaita, which says there is one highest ultimate reality, that is the formless and attribute-less Brahman. There is no duality, hence there is nothing other than that Brahman. The world and living beings are seen and experienced through the mind and senses. Brahman is beyond both. From that point of view, the world is like a dream.

Polytheism merely refers to image and idol worship of various different gods that are not aspects of one underlying reality or God. There is no polytheism in any of the world's great religions. It was there in pre-Judaic times and in pre-Islamic times in Mecca and surrounding religions. It was never there in Hinduism. Pantheism is different from polytheism and says the same God is manifest in everything in the universe.

Thus we see that there are various concepts of God. The following table is not precise, since the western and Indian concepts of God differ, and each of the terms— monotheism, pantheism, immanent God and transcendent reality—are interpreted differently by various scholars.

	Monotheism—Highest reality without form, without attributes	Monotheism—God without form but with attributes	Pantheism
Dualism—God separate from living beings and matter		Judaism, Christianity and Islam; Dvaita philosophy in Hinduism	Idol and image worship in Hinduism—knowing each represents one facet of One God
Immanent—God in matter and living beings		One aspect of Sikhism	One aspect of Visishtadvaita philosophy in Hinduism
Transcendent—beyond space, time, causation	Advaita philosophy in Hinduism; can argue this is similar to Buddhism and Jainism		Another aspect of Visishtadvaita philosophy in Hinduism

Concepts of God are not antagonistic, they are complementary. People have different temperaments. For instance, devotees or worshippers of God think of God as separate from them. God could be formless, as in the Abrahamic religions, or with various forms, as in Hinduism. Either way, God protects, gives rewards and is a source of security. Some feel they are a part of God.

Those who think there is an ultimate reality beyond form, attributes, space, time and causation accept the Advaita, Buddhist or Jain philosophy. In such a conception, the individual is the same as that ultimate reality.

In the final analysis, it comes down to whether matter is everything or whether there is something beyond matter. If matter is everything, then consciousness, human feelings and so on are products of matter and how it combines and recombines, and there is nothing beyond it. In modern philosophy, one view is that consciousness is the product of neurological and chemical processes. Both Buddhism and Jainism, which reject the notion of God as creator, explicitly say that they are not nihilistic and do not accept this. The major religions of the world say that there is indeed something beyond matter, which we can call God, spirit, Atman or consciousness. Even Buddha says 'because there is an unborn, unbecome, unmade, unconditioned, therefore you do know an escape from the born, become, made and conditioned.' (Tatiyanibbānasuttaṁ 8-3)

There is a way of reconciling various aspects of God or the state beyond mind and matter. When we identify too much with the body, then God is out there as creator and lord of the universe. When we identify more with the mind than with the body, we say that God is within us. Various religions also say this. Judaism says, 'I (Yahweh) have said, Ye are gods; and all of you are children of the most High'– Psalm 82:6. Jesus says that 'The Kingdom of God is within you'. The Quran tells us 'It is We who created humankind and fully know what their souls whisper to them, and We are closer to them than their jugular vein' (Quran 50:16). All Indian religions except Buddhism say there is a soul within us. Buddhism, however, says 'be aware', and in Hinduism, awareness comes from consciousness, which is the very nature of God or the soul. If we go beyond the body and mind and identify with the soul, then we think of ourselves as one with God. Jesus says, 'My father and I are one.' The Sufi saint Mansur Al-hallaj said 'Anal Haq' or I am the truth. The Upanishads say '*Aham Brahmasmi*' and '*Ayam Atma Brahma*', meaning 'The Self is the same as Brahman (the ultimate reality)'.

Concluding Remarks

It is not possible for one religion to ultimately prevail and eliminate all other religions. The reason is that human beings have different temperaments, religious needs and aspirations. The very existence of so many religions and sects within a religion point to this truth. One religion cannot meet everyone's needs. Each highlights some aspects of the truth. Vivekananda said, 'The end seems, therefore, to be not destruction but a multiplication of sects until each individual is a sect unto himself.'[2]

NOTES

Preface

1   *Sri Ramakrishna and His Unique Message*, Swami Ghananda, Advaita Ashrama, India 1969, in Foreword by Arnold Toynbee
2   Trilochan Sastry, *The Essentials of Hinduism* (Penguin Random House India, 2023)

Introduction

1   Encyclopaedia Britannica
2   *Mysticism*, Christian Classics Ethereal Library Description: First published in 1911
3   C. G. Jung, J. Campbell and others were modern psychologists and scholars who studied myths. Jung has the theory of a collective subconscious through which symbols emerge. These symbols form the basis of myths. The individual finds meaning in these myths.

Chapter 3: Islam

1   Polygamy was perhaps prevalent worldwide and not only in the regions around Jerusalem and Mecca. In India, the king

Dasarath, father of Rama, a Hindu incarnation of the God Vishnu had three wives. Lord Krishna, another incarnation of Vishnu, has several wives. The Pandavas or five brothers in the Mahabharata, also had more than one wife. In fact, Draupadi had five husbands.

2   Compared to Islam, the Gospels in Christianity were compiled between 66 CE and 100 CE, three or more decades after the passing away of Jesus Christ. The words of the Buddha were recorded similarly, two or more decades after his passing away. The Quran was compiled and a final version was available within two decades of the passing away of Prophet Mohammad.

3   Ibn Abbas was considered the greatest author, scholar and elucidator of the Quran, respected by both Sunnis and Shias. He was reported to have said that syllables like Alif-Lal-Meem have a meaning. He was a cousin of the Prophet, heard the Quran from him directly and also received teachings from him in person.

4   Verses referring to the spirit of Allah are given here. 'I will fashion out for you a creation out of clay after the manner of a bird, then I will breathe into it a new spirit and it will become a soaring being by the command of Allah' (Surah 3:49). Surah 5:39: 'You breathed into it a new spirit', 'And remember when the Lord said to the angels, "I am about to create man from dry clay, from black mud wrought into shape; So when I have fashioned him in perfection and have breathed into him of My Spirit, fall ye down in submission to him"' (Surah 15: 28-29). 'Then He fashioned him and breathed into him of His spirit' (Surah 32:9), 'When thy Lord said to the angels, "I am about to create man from clay, And so when I have fashioned him in perfection, and have breathed into him of My Spirit, fall ye down in submission to him"' (Surah 38:71-72).

5   Sufi saints continue to be revered even in places like India, which is predominantly Hindu. The reverence is shown by pilgrimages to the tombs of the Sufi saints. For instance, the dargah or tomb of Moinuddin Chisti, a thirteenth century mystic in Ajmer, India, is visited by several tens of thousands of pilgrims daily. Other such pilgrimage spots are in Pakistan, Bangladesh, Turkey, Egypt, Senegal and Kazakhstan.

Chapter 4: Buddhism

1   The Eight Fold Path comprises *samma ditti* (right view), *samma sankalpa* (right thought), *samma vacha* (right speech), *samma kammanta* (right action), *sammajiva* (right livelihood), *samma vāyāma* (right endeavour), *samma sati* (right mindfulness) and *samma samadhi* (right concentration).

2   The Mundaka (Mundaka 3.1.6) Upanishad says, 'Truth alone wins, not falsehood; by truth, the *Devayanah* (the path of the Devas) is widened, that by which the seers travel on, having nothing to wish for to where there is that—the highest treasure attained by truth.'

Chapter 5: Jainism

1   The twenty-four Tirthankaras are Rishabh Nath, Ajita, Shambhava, Abhinandana, Sumati, Padmaprabha, Suparshva, Chandraprabha, Pushpadanta, Shitala, Shreyamsha, Vasupujya, Vimala, Ananta, Dharma, Shanti, Kunthu, Ara, Malli, Suvrata, Nami, Arishtanemi, Parshvanath, Vardhaman or Mahavira. Even today, there are temples of the Tirthankaras.

2   There are interesting stories about the birth of the founders of some religions. Mahavira's mother had divine dreams

foretelling a great birth. Buddha's mother had a vision where a white elephant entered her right side, after which she became pregnant. The Holy Spirit entered Mary and she gave birth to Jesus. The birth of the Prophet Mohammad was predicted by Jesus over six centuries earlier, according to the Quran.

3   According to Digambara Jain texts, the emperor Chandragupta Maurya renounced his kingdom and followed the monk Bhadrabahu to south India. The Svetambara Jains have a different version, where Chandragupta died in north India

4   This is one issue on which the Indian religions differ. Buddhism does not give the status of reality to anything. In Hinduism, there are many views—some which agree with some aspects of Jainism, and some with some aspects of Buddhism.

5   The intermarriage between Jains and one Hindu caste indicates that it is likely that in ancient times, many of the Hindus who accepted Jainism came from the merchant or business caste. It is also likely that the Brahmin-dominated Hindu religion did not give them a proper place in the religion. Jainism offered that.

Chapter 7: Hindusm

1   Swami Vivekananda, *The Complete Works of Swami Vivekananda, Vol 1*, https://www.ramakrishnavivekananda. info/vivekananda/complete_works.htm

2   Bhagavad Gita, Chapter 18

3   Swami Vivekananda, *The Complete Works of Swami Vivekananda, Vol 4*, https://www.ramakrishnavivekananda. info/vivekananda/complete_works.htm

4   Swami Vivekananda, *The Complete Works of Swami Vivekananda, Vol 5*, https://www.ramakrishnavivekananda. info/vivekananda/complete_works.htm

Chapter 8: Harmony of World Religions

1   Swami Vivekananda, *The Complete Works of Swami Vivekananda*, *Vol 1*, https://www.ramakrishnavivekananda. info/vivekananda/complete_works.htm
2   Swami Vivekananda, *The Complete Works of Swami Vivekananda*, *Vol 4*, https://www.ramakrishnavivekananda. info/vivekananda/complete_works.htm

Scan QR code to access the
Penguin Random House India website